Sonoma County Bike Trails

Third Edition

Easy to Challenging Bicycle Rides
for Touring and Mountain Bikes

D0033522

By Phyllis L. Neumann
Author of *Marin County Bike Trails*

Illustrations by Mary H. Dicke

Penngrove Publications
P.O. Box 1017
Penngrove, California 94951
http://www.penngrovepub.com

To Bob, Cindy, and Andrea,
whose encouragement and support
made this book possible

"I would rather be ashes than dust!" by Jack London
Reprinted by permission of Milo Shepard, executor of the Jack London estate.

"Grapes" by Alexander Pushkin
From THE POEMS AND PROSE OF PUSHKIN, edited by Avrahm Yarmolinsky. Copyright 1936 and renewed 1964 by Random House, Inc. Reprinted by permission of Random House, Inc.

"Once by the Pacific" by Robert Frost
From THE POETRY OF ROBERT FROST, edited by Edward Connery Lathem. Copyright 1916, 1928 © 1969 by Holt, Rinehart and Winston. Copyright 1944, © 1956 by Robert Frost. Reprinted by permission of Holt, Rinehart and Winston, Publishers.

"Pastoral" by Edna St. Vincent Millay
From COLLECTED POEMS, Harper & Row. Copyright 1921, 1948 by Edna St. Vincent Millay.

SONOMA COUNTY BIKE TRAILS, Third Edition
Copyright © 1999 by PENNGROVE PUBLICATIONS
ISBN 0-9621694-7-1

All rights reserved. No part of this book may be reproduced in any form or by any means without prior written permission of the publisher.

Printed in the United States of America

First printing, February 1978
Second Edition, June 1989
Third Edition, June 1999
Fourteenth printing, October 2001

Cover photograph by Jeff Dooley
Taken looking northeast on Red Winery Road in Geyserville
Cyclists: Cindy Neumann and Marshall Vincent

Penngrove Publications
P.O. Box 1017
Penngrove, California 94951
www.penngrovepub.com

TABLE OF CONTENTS

Introduction

Explore Sonoma County by Bike! . . . 1
Some Tips for Better Touring . . . 2
How to Use This Book . . . 3
Sonoma County Map . . . 4
Regions of Sonoma County . . . 5
Calendar of Sonoma County Annual Events . . . 6

Road Rides . . . 9

I. Southern Sonoma County . . . *9*
1. Petaluma to the Cheese Factory . . . 10
2. Cotati to Bloomfield . . . 13
3. Penngrove Area Loop Trip . . . 16

II. The Sonoma Valley "Valley of the Moon" . . . 19
4. City of Sonoma Historic Ramble . . . 20
5. Sonoma to Glen Ellen . . . 24
6. Glen Ellen to Kenwood . . . 27

III. Northern Sonoma County . . . *30*
7. Healdsburg — Dry Creek Valley . . . 31
8. Geyserville — Alexander Valley Wine Tour . . . 33
9. Cloverdale to Asti . . . 36

IV. The Russian River Region . . . *39*
10. Guerneville to Armstrong Woods . . . 40
11. Guerneville — River Road Ride . . . 43
12. Healdsburg — Eastside, Westside Loop . . . 46
13. Monte Rio to Cazadero . . . 49

V. The Coastal Region . . . *53*
14. Bodega to Bodega Head . . . 54
15. Tomales to Valley Ford . . . 58
16. Occidental to the Coast *"The Coleman Valley Experience"* . . . 61

VI. The Santa Rosa Area . . . *65*
17. Howarth Park to Spring Lake . . . 66
18. Bennett Valley Loop Trip . . . 69
19. Santa Rosa — Mark West Springs Loop . . . 72

VII. The Sebastopol Area . . . *76*
20. Lone Pine Road Loop Trip . . . 77
21. Freestone – Valley Ford – Bloomfield Triangle . . . 80
22. Occidental to Freestone . . . 83

Mountain Bike Rides . . . 86

State and Regional Parks in Sonoma County . . . *86*
23. Santa Rosa — Annadel State Park . . . 88
24. Rohnert Park — Crane Creek Regional Park . . . 91
25. Windsor — Foothill/Shiloh Regional Parks . . . 94
26. Petaluma — Helen Putnam Regional Park . . . 98
27. Sebastopol — West County and Joe Rodota Trails . . . 101
28. Occidental — Willow Creek Ride . . . 103

Highway 101 Access Route — Cloverdale to Petaluma . . . 106

Appendix

Rides by Ratings . . . 111
Bicycle Shops in Sonoma County . . . 112
Points of Interest . . . 113

ACKNOWLEDGMENTS

All books need the help of good friends and family to stimulate and encourage such a large undertaking. I could not have written this book without it. Therefore, in warmest appreciation I wish to thank:

SANDY AND LAMOYNE FRANK, who first discussed the idea with me about writing a bicycle touring book, and gave me the support and energy I needed as well as many of their own hours, I extend my sincere thanks.

STEVE AND NANCY PHILLIPS. To Steve, for the generous use of his aircraft altimeter; and to Nancy, for her companionship on many of the rides and her helpful critique of the book.

JOHN AND JAN GILMAN. To John, for his help in riding and writing a couple of the trips; and to Jan, for her beautiful photographs.

TOM FOREMAN AND LOUISE COOLEY, for their time and expertise in editing the book.

BARBARA LINDE, for her tireless effort and determination in helping to get the book promoted. My sincere appreciation.

RAWLS FRAZIER, for writing of the Highway 101 Access Route from Cloverdale to Petaluma, as well the mountain bike rides. He was also invaluable in checking and edited the rides before each new printing. Thanks, Rawls.

A very special appreciation to my husband, BOB, for his frank and helpful criticism, his proofreading and editing, and his constant encouragement and support in working on the book, as well as his companionship on many of the rides.

A special thank you to my daughters, CINDY and ANDREA, for their forbearance and support through so many busy hours.

And to the many others whose ideas and opinions helped to make this book possible, I offer my sincerest gratitude.

Photo credits are given to:

JEFF DOOLEY — cover, page 63
KAY FIELD — page 82
JAN GILMAN — pages 1, 11, 15, 23, 26, 28, 29, 42, 51, 52, 56, 68, 71, 74, 75, 85
CINDY NEUMANN — pages 18, 22, 44, 59, 60, 78, 81
PHYLLIS NEUMANN — page 12
CHATEAU SOUVERAIN — page 34
RAWLS FRAZIER — pages 38, 89, 95, 96, 99, 105

GOING DOWN HILL ON A BICYCLE

With lifted feet, hands still
I am poised, and down the hill
Dart, with heedful mind;
The air goes by in a wind.

Swifter and yet more swift,
Till the heart with a mighty lift
Makes the lungs laugh, the throat cry: —
"O bird, see; see, bird, I fly."

"Is this, is this your joy?
O bird then I, though a boy,
For a golden moment share
Your feathery life in air!"

Say, heart, is there aught like this
In a world that is full of bliss?
'Tis more than skating, bound
Steel-shod to the level ground.

Speed slackens now, I float
Awhile in my airy boat;
Till, when the wheels scarce crawl,
My feet to the treadles fall.

Alas, that the longest hill
Must end in a vale; but still,
Who climbs with toil, wheresoe'er,
Shall find wings waiting there.

—Henry Charles Beeching

EXPLORE SONOMA COUNTY BY BIKE!

One of the best places for bicycling is *SONOMA* COUNTY, with its tranquil country roads, gently rolling farmlands, towering redwoods, lush vineyards, and breathtaking coastline. This is an ideal area for spending many glorious days on your bike, exploring the diverse regions that make this county so unique and enjoyable.

Sonoma County is about an hour's drive from San Francisco, 40 miles north of the Golden Gate Bridge on Highway 101. It extends inland to the town of Sonoma and westward to the coast. Its moderate climate makes bicycling enjoyable the year round, and especially pleasant during the summer months when there's absolutely no rain. Depending upon your mood, you can select a wide variety of terrain and climate for a bike trip. The coast is mountainous, fairly cool, often quite foggy and can even get a bit blustery. As you move inland toward the valleys, the cliffs give way to gently rolling hills and the weather softens and brightens into sunny blue skies with tranquil breezes and warmer temperatures. The northern area boasts of its incredible towering redwoods, famous wineries and the Russian River; while the southern area is somewhat more agricultural, known for its large dairy farms and vast orchards. No matter what region you select for your trip you can be assured of good cycling with fantastic scenery.

Being relatively new to biking, my friends and I were surprised and exhilarated by the quaint country roads we discovered only minutes from home. We felt as if we had stepped into a painting — the kind you only seem to find in jigsaw puzzles. The riding on these back roads was safe, easy, and yet exciting. We began exploring more of the county when we discovered bike racks and transported our bikes to recommended locations. Local bike enthusiasts all had their own ideas of the best bike routes to take. We tried them and incorporated many of our favorites into this book. The ones with too much traffic or too little scenery were discarded. We did include some especially beautiful, but challenging, rides for more ambitious or experienced riders. In all, there are over *450 miles* of biking trails in this book — enough to keep you on the road for quite a while!

Sonoma County Bike Trails has been written with the casual cyclist in mind — the person or family that wants to take advantage of the lush and varied Sonoma County countryside and to stop along the way at interesting spots for a picnic, a wine tour, some sightseeing, or just a breather. We could have used a book like this when we were getting started. We hope you can use it now!

HAPPY BICYCLING!

Phyllis Neumann

SOME TIPS FOR BETTER TOURING

All bicyclists have individual needs, depending upon their riding styles, degrees of experience, and personalities. A beginner cannot keep pace with an experienced cyclist, and therefore shouldn't try. He needs more frequent rest stops and gentler grades to keep him from having a miserable time, defeating the purpose of a pleasant day's outing. We learned that the hard way. We nearly burned ourselves out one day in our efforts to keep pace with an active cycling club whose typical morning warm-up rides were over 35 miles! We struggled to keep up for quite a while and were just about ready to pack it in when we decided to forget the club and take it at our own pace. We began talking to each other again, instead of frantically grinding away at the pedals; and we focused once again on the scenery, realizing that we had forgotten that it even existed. The trip took over an hour longer to complete (everyone had gone home), but it taught us a good lesson and renewed our faith in bicycling.

How can you improve your riding efficiency? Experienced cyclists develop a rhythm and pedal at a relatively constant rate of speed. This is called *cadence* and is measured in crank revolutions per minute (rpm). Each individual has a natural cadence which feels most comfortable for him. Casual cyclists seem to develop a cadence rate between 55-75 rpm; whereas serious cyclists establish a cadence somewhere between 100-140 rpm. Beginners often tend to pedal too slowly. Count your pedal strokes per minute. If your rate is much below 60 rpm, try pedaling faster by switching to a lower gear to maintain a good average pace.

The most common mistake beginners make is to start off with a burst of speed in the morning and then burn out before noon. It is more efficient to keep up a steady rhythm, mile after mile, uphill or down, rather than to use the "pedal-coast" style of riding. The body works best when it builds up stamina evenly and gradually instead of in short spurts, thereby tiring less quickly.

The gears on a 10-speed bicycle permit you to maintain your most efficient natural cadence, regardless of most terrain. When pedaling becomes too easy and there is little pedal resistance, shift to a higher gear; when it gets too difficult to maintain cadence, shift to a lower gear. (Of course, there are times when nothing helps. Those are the times to get off and hike it!)

A note of interest for you calorie-counters: Moderate cycling uses up an average of 5 calories per minute, or 300 calories per hour. Vigorous cycling, the kind you do going up a hill, uses up approximately 10 calories per minute, or 600 calories per hour. Therefore, in a 3-hour trip you can easily use up over 1,000 calories — provided that you don't stop at the nearest restaurant and gorge yourself when the ride is over! *(3500 calories = 1 pound)*

HOW TO USE THIS BOOK

The way people take a bike trip covers a wide range of needs and speeds. This book is for people who are comfortable with rides where the looking and the touring are just as important as the pedaling. Many of the rides are around 20 miles long. There are short, easy rides for families with small children, and challenging rides for those out for a day's adventure.

Even a 20-mile ride can have varying degrees of difficulty and can be taken at a multitude of speeds. The variables seem to depend upon individual capabilities, equipment, weather conditions, terrain, or just how you feel that day and who you're with.

THE RIDING TIME specified in the book is to be used only as a flexible guide. It does not take into account rest stops or sightseeing. In general, you can estimate your own riding time as follows:

5 - 10 miles per hour	beginning or inexperienced riders traveling at a casual, leisurely pace.
10 - 20 miles per hour	good, strong riders traveling at a moderate pace
20 - 30 miles per hour	serious cyclists in good condition traveling at a steady, brisk pace

THE RIDES have all been designed as loop trips, in that they end at the same place they begin without retracing their path. No pickup car is needed. They have been rated as **easy, medium,** or **challenging.**

An easy ride is one that is relatively short (10 miles or less), has easy or few grades, and can be ridden by beginners and children of all ages.

A medium ride is usually a bit longer (10-25 miles), and may include some moderate grades, though none too strenuous or too steep.

A challenging ride is for experienced riders (or ambitious ones). It is not geared for everyone, and will exhaust the beginner or novice rider. The grades are steep (walk-ups) and there may be several of them. These trips usually take at least half a day to complete without stops, and generally measure 20 miles or longer.

MAPS of the ride indicate the route to be ridden in strong, bold lines, while the adjoining roads are marked in lighter lines. Variations and extensions of the ride are indicated by broken lines. Interesting places to stop are also noted on the map, as well as nearby bike shops for repairs. The arrow shows you where to begin and in what direction.

ELEVATION PROFILES were taken for each trip, and were recorded at ½-mile intervals. They are invaluable in giving a picture of the terrain and will help you to determine whether the trip is more (or less) difficult than you want to tackle that day.

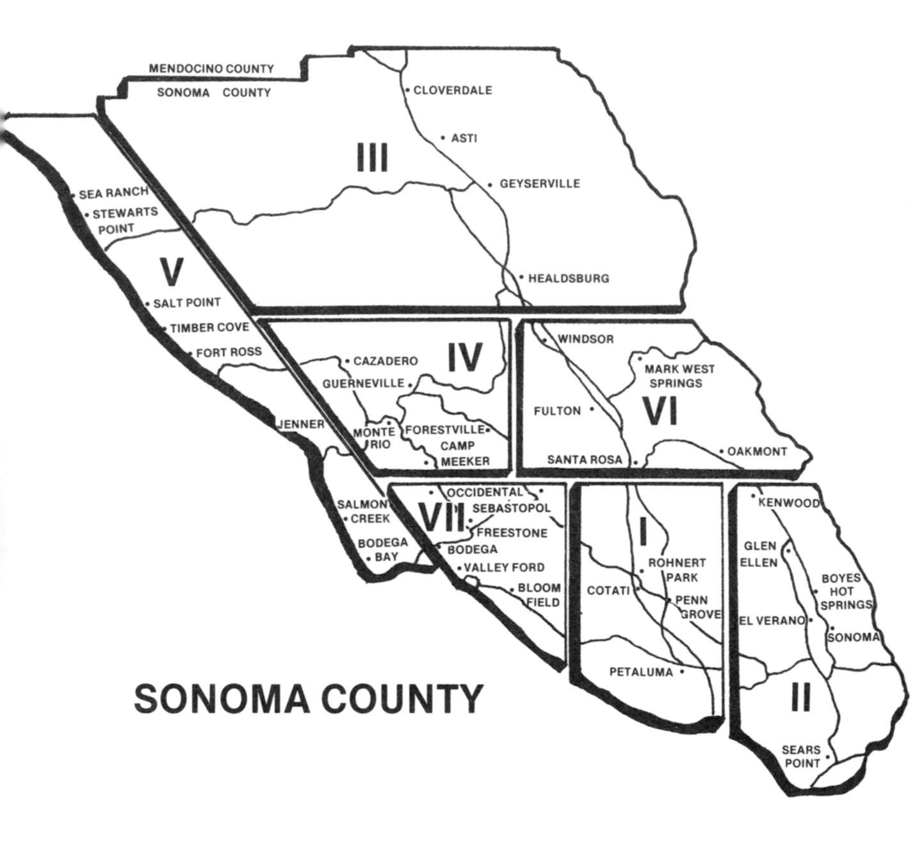
MENDOCINO COUNTY
SONOMA COUNTY
CLOVERDALE
ASTI
III
GEYSERVILLE
SEA RANCH
STEWARTS POINT
V
HEALDSBURG
SALT POINT
TIMBER COVE
FORT ROSS
WINDSOR
CAZADERO
IV
MARK WEST SPRINGS
GUERNEVILLE
FULTON
VI
JENNER
MONTE RIO
FORESTVILLE
CAMP MEEKER
SANTA ROSA
OAKMONT
OCCIDENTAL
SALMON CREEK
VII
SEBASTOPOL
KENWOOD
FREESTONE
I
BODEGA BAY
BODEGA
GLEN ELLEN
ROHNERT PARK
VALLEY FORD
BOYES HOT SPRINGS
COTATI
BLOOM FIELD
PENN GROVE
EL VERANO
SONOMA
PETALUMA
II
SONOMA COUNTY
SEARS POINT

REGIONS OF SONOMA COUNTY

I. SOUTHERN SONOMA COUNTY

Beautiful agricultural setting of fertile plains and rolling hills. Famous for its poultry industry, Petaluma was once considered to be "The Egg Capital of the World." The area's large dairy farms still serve much of the bay area.

II. THE SONOMA VALLEY "Valley of the Moon"

Richly endowed with much of California's early history and magnificent old wineries. The valley's orchards, vineyards, and steaming hot springs make this area a landmark. Jack London's beautiful "Valley of the Moon" is visible from his old home in Glen Ellen.

III. NORTHERN SONOMA COUNTY

The heart of wine country. Many excellent wineries surround this area, and lush fertile vineyards and orchards stretch out for miles. The beauty of the countryside is at its height in March, when prune trees are in bloom.

IV. THE RUSSIAN RIVER REGION

Famous for being Sonoma County's recreational playland. Resort communities line the Russian River in a fantastic setting of redwoods, vineyards, and orchards.

V. THE COASTAL REGION

Some of the most magnificent and breathtaking coastline in the world. Coastal bluffs, steep slopes giving way to fields of grazing sheep, and numerous beach coves offer majestically rugged beauty overlooking the vast Pacific Ocean.

VI. THE SANTA ROSA AREA

Santa Rosa, the county seat and largest city in Sonoma County, offers some excellent bike trails within its city limits. Just outside its busy hub you will find rolling hills and a panoramic countryside.

VII. THE SEBASTOPOL AREA

Nestled in beautiful rolling farmlands dotted with oak, eucalyptus, and redwood groves, as well as miles of orchards. Sebastopol is known for its Gravenstein apples. The trees are exquisite around Easter when the blossoms are at their peak, and again in August when the apples are ripe and ready for picking.

CALENDAR OF SONOMA COUNTY ANNUAL EVENTS (1999)

Use this calendar to coordinate your ride with local events.

JANUARY

CLOVERDALE	***Old-Time Fiddler's Contest & Festival.*** Citrus Fairgrounds. 1st weekend in January.

FEBRUARY

CLOVERDALE	***Cloverdale Citrus Fair.*** Citrus Fairgrounds. Washington's Birthday weekend, Fri-Mon 10-10 p.m. (707) 894-3992

MARCH

PETALUMA	***Spring Craft Fair.*** Petaluma Community Center. 1st weekend in March, 10-4 p.m. (707) 778-4380

APRIL

BODEGA BAY	***Fisherman's Festival.*** FREE. Bodega Yacht Club. 2nd weekend in April, 10-4 p.m. (707) 875-3422
PETALUMA	***Butter & Egg Days Parade.*** Downtown Petaluma. Last Saturday in April, 12 p.m.. (707) 762-9348
PETALUMA	***Opening Day of the Petaluma River.*** Downtown River Harbor. 3rd weekend in April, 3 p.m. (707) 765-6750
SEBASTOPOL	***Apple Blossom Festival.*** Parade on Saturday. Ives Park. 3rd weekend in April. 12 p.m. (707) 823-3032

MAY

CLOVERDALE	***May Festival & Parade.*** Citrus Fairgrounds. 2nd Friday-Sunday of May, 10-10 p.m. Parade Saturday.
HEALDSBURG	***Memorial Day Weekend Antique Fair.*** FREE. Healdsburg Plaza, 9-4 p.m. (707) 433-4315
MONTE RIO	***Summer Soundfest.*** Monte Rio Amphitheater. 3rd Saturday in May. (707) 869-1808
PETALUMA	***Art in the Park.*** FREE. Walnut Park. 10-5 p.m.
PETALUMA	***Annual Human Race.*** 3K and 10K walk, run or ride your bike to benefit Hospice. (707) 778-6242
PETALUMA	***Living History Day.*** Petaluma Adobe State Park. Mid Saturday in May, 10-5 p.m. (707) 769-0429
SANTA ROSA	***Human Race.*** 3K and 10K walk, run or ride your bike to raise funds. (707) 544-1581
SANTA ROSA	***Luther Burbank Rose Parade Festival.*** FREE. Downtown. 2nd weekend in May. (707) 542-7673
SONOMA	***Cinco de Mayo Celebration.*** Sonoma Plaza. (707) 938-4626

JUNE

DUNCANS MILLS	***Russian River Rodeo Parade & BBQ.*** Downtown Duncans Mills. 1st weekend in June. (707) 869-1959
DUNCANS MILLS	***Festival of the Arts.*** Downtown Duncans Mills. 2nd weekend in June. (707) 824-8404
GUERNEVILLE	***Stumptown Daze.*** Parade, BBQ and rodeo. FREE. Field. 2nd week in June. (800) 253-8800
GUERNEVILLE	***Russian River Blues Festival.*** Johnson's Beach. 3rd weekend in June. (510) 655-9471
PETALUMA	***Sonoma-Marin Fair.*** Petaluma Fairgrounds. 3rd week in June, 12 p.m.-12 a.m.
SONOMA	***Annual Ox Roast.*** Sonoma Plaza. 1st Sunday in June. (707) 938-4626
SONOMA	***Flag Day Celebration.*** Sonoma Plaza. 2nd Sunday in June. (707) 938-3681
SONOMA	***Annual Arts & Show.*** Sonoma Plaza. 1st weekend in June. 10-5 p.m. (707) 453-1656
SONOMA	***Father's Day Turkey Barbecue.*** Sonoma Plaza. (707) 996-3094

JULY

HEALDSBURG	***Annual Harvest Century Bicycle Tour.*** 22.5, 37 or 62.1 mile route along Alexander, Russian River and Dry Creek Valleys. (800) 648-9922
HEALDSBURG	***Concert Series in the Park.*** FREE. Healdsburg Plaza. July and August. 2-4 p.m. (707) 433-6935
KENWOOD	***4th of July Celebration & Parade.*** Downtown Kenwood. 7:30-5 p.m. (707) 833-2440
MONTE RIO	***Rocky Beach Games & Water Parade.*** 1st weekend in July. 12 p.m. (707) 865-2487
RIO NIDO	***4th of July BBQ.*** Downtown Rio Nido. 12 p.m. (707) 869-2326
SANTA ROSA	***Sonoma County Fair.*** Sonoma County Fairgrounds. Last week of July, 1st week of August. (707) 545-4200
SONOMA	***4th of July Parade & Plaza Celebration.*** FREE. Sonoma Plaza. (707) 938-4626
SONOMA	***Annual Salute to the Arts.*** Sonoma Plaza. Last Saturday in July. 10-6 p.m. (707) 938-2133
WINDSOR	***Founders Day.*** Children's games, food, music, fireworks. (707) 838-1260

AUGUST

COTATI	***Indian Summer Festival.*** Cotati Plaza, 11-6 p.m.
HEALDSBURG	***Concert Series in the Park.*** FREE. Healdsburg Plaza. July and August. 2-4 p.m. (707) 433-6935

PETALUMA — ***Old Adobe Fiesta and Outdoor Art Show.*** Old Adobe Historic Park. 3rd Sunday in August.

SANTA ROSA — ***Sonoma County Fair.*** Sonoma County Fairgrounds. Last week of July, 1st week of August. (707) 545-4200

SEBASTOPOL — ***Gravenstein Apple Fair.*** Ragle Ranch Park. 2nd weekend in August, 10-6 p.m. (707) 571-8288

SEPTEMBER

GRATON — ***Graton Day.*** FREE. Downtown Graton. Afternoon. (707) 829-3716

GUERNEVILLE — ***Russian River Jazz Festival.*** Johnson's Beach. 2nd weekend in September. (707) 869-3940

JENNER — ***A Whale of a Gala.*** 1st weekend in September. (707) 865-2689

SONOMA — ***Valley of the Moon Vintage Festival.*** Sonoma Plaza. Last weekend in September. (707) 996-2109

OCTOBER

SANTA ROSA — ***Sonoma County Harvest Fair.*** Sonoma County Fairgrounds. 1st weekend in October. (707) 545-4203

DECEMBER

CLOVERDALE — ***Holiday Craft Fair.*** Citrus Fairgrounds. 1st weekend in December.

SANTA ROSA — ***Spirit of Christmas Crafts Fair.*** Sonoma County Fairgrounds. 1st and 2nd weekend in December.

ONGOING EVENTS

ALEXANDER VALLEY — ***1st Weekend in Alexander Valley.*** Monthly series of special events. FREE. 11-3 p.m. (707) 431-2894

JENNER — ***View Harbor Seal Pups at Goat Rock.*** Sonoma Coast State Beach. March-September. (707) 865-3127

PETALUMA — ***Petaluma Adobe State Historic Park.*** Daily demos in cooking, weaving, candle-making. (707) 762-4871

PETALUMA — ***Petaluma Farmers Market.*** Walnut Park. Ongoing Saturdays, 2-5 p.m. (707) 762-0344

SANTA ROSA — ***Sonoma County Museum.*** Wednesday and Sundays, 11-4 p.m. (707) 579-1500

SANTA ROSA — ***Pacific Coast Air Museum.*** 3rd Saturday of every month, 10-4 p.m. (707) 575-7900

SONOMA — ***Sonoma Valley Friday Farmer's Market.*** FREE. Depot Park. Year-round, 9-12 (707) 538-7023

SONOMA COAST COUNTY BEACHES — ***Whale Watching.*** January-April. Bodega Bay, Bodega Head, Fort Ross and Salt Point. (707) 869-9177

I. SOUTHERN SONOMA COUNTY

A FARM PICTURE

Through the ample open door of the peaceful country barn,
A sunlit pasture field with cattle and horses feeding,
And haze and vista, and the far horizon fading away.

WALT WHITMAN

1 PETALUMA TO THE CHEESE FACTORY

REGION: ***SOUTHERN SONOMA COUNTY***

MILEAGE: *21.5 MILES (3 - 4 HOURS RIDING TIME)*

RATING: *CHALLENGING RIDE — A scenic route along country roads with picturesque rolling hills and peaceful dairy farms. Several difficult climbs make this trip a struggle, but worth the effort.*

ROUTE: *Take "D" Street from Walnut Park and follow it directly to the Cheese Factory. Backtrack about a mile and turn left on Wilson-Hill Road. Turn right on Chileno Valley Road and right again on Western Avenue. This road will take you back to Petaluma. Turn right on Howard Street, left on "D" Street back to Walnut Park.*

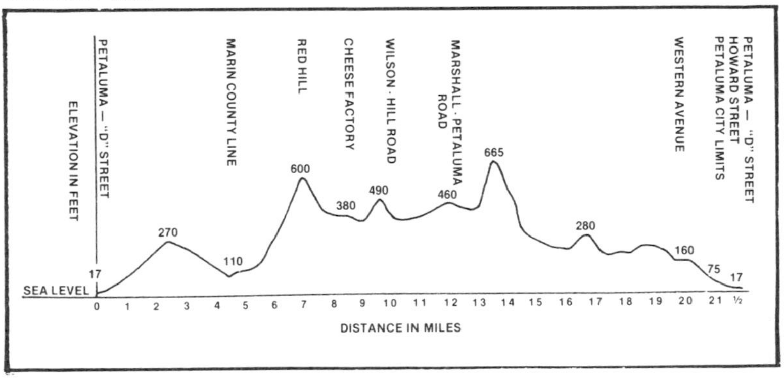

Begin your trip at Walnut Park, located at "D" Street in downtown Petaluma. Noted for its egg and poultry production, Petaluma has been known for years as the "World's Egg Basket." It is also a major dairy industry center and an inland port at the head of the Petaluma River, connecting Southern Sonoma County with San Francisco Bay.

"D" Street emphasizes the charm and quaintness of the town and takes you through Petaluma's most elegant neighborhood, lined with expensive vintage homes and small estates. A moderate climb marks the outskirts of the city and exposes miles of scenic dairyland punctuated by rolling hills and grazing cattle. Occasional cars and trucks use these country roads, but usually the air is filled with singing birds and gentle breezes. The several climbs begin briskly enough but only last ½ mile or so before descending. You will cross a concrete bridge marking the entrance to Marin County. A sign tells you that the road curves for 2 miles. It means just that — it feels as if it is going straight up. This is *Red Hill*. There are frequent turnouts for breathers which overlook vast valleys and old dairy farms.

Some 9 miles further on a white arrow appears on your right pointing the way toward *The Cheese Factory*. Just over a small hill and you are there. *The Cheese Factory* is a charming place, full of the aromas of freshly made cheeses. The quaint store offers samplings of cheeses, as well as other deli treats. Their delicious home-made buttermilk is a great thirst-quencher. You can eat lunch by a lovely pond alive with ducks and geese. A number of picnic tables are set up for the occasion. Tours of the factory are offered every 15 minutes throughout the day. The tour takes 10-15 minutes and leads you through the cool chambers where the cheeses are processed.

On your return trip, backtrack about 1 mile until you see a sign pointing the way to Petaluma, 8 miles. This road runs north and is fairly hilly. At the intersection, 2½ miles from this point, a sign warns of loose gravel. This marks an ascent that is very strenuous and steep and will poop out the most eager biker. If you look down, you can see the road you just were on — 200 feet below you. The climb is worth the struggle and sweat, for a successful ascent rewards you with a panoramic landscape that can be fully appreciated on the effortless coast down. Once you are down, look for Western Avenue, turn right and follow it back to downtown Petaluma, about 4 blocks north of "D" Street. Turn right on Howard Street to "D" Street, turn left 2 blocks to Walnut Park and your car.

The Great Petaluma Mill, down the street, is an interesting place to browse when you are through. It is a complex of new stores and craft shops on the Petaluma River that have been converted from an old grain mill.

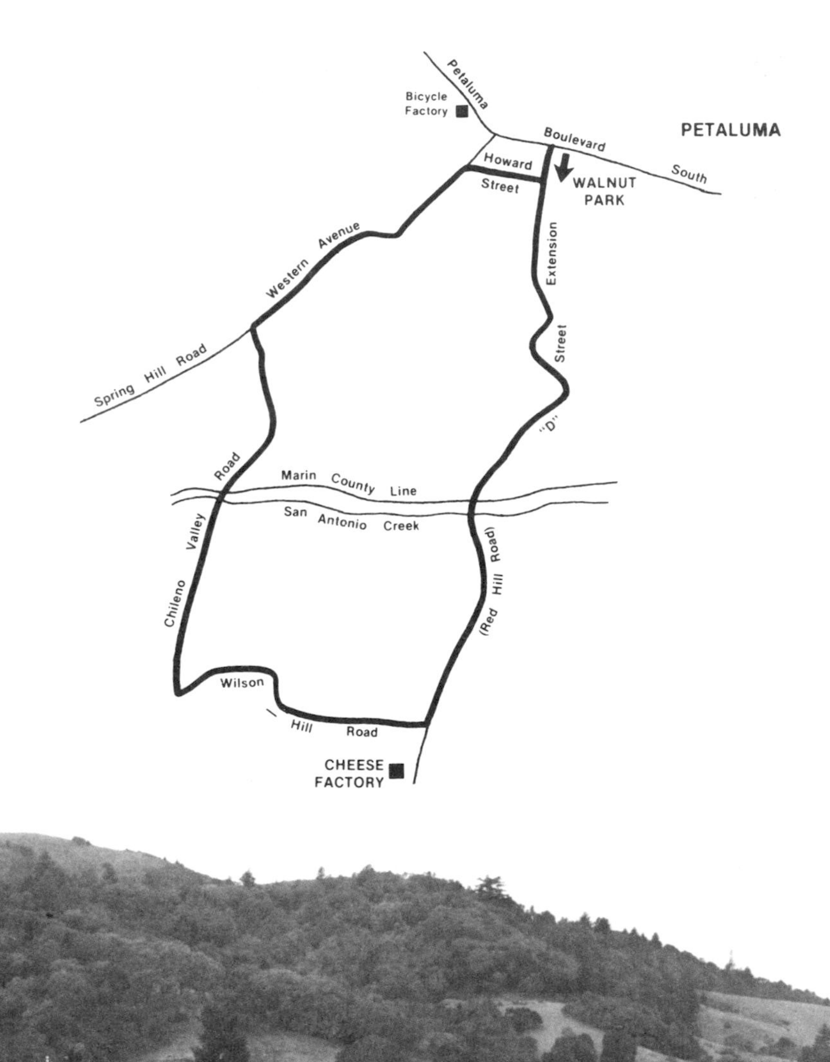
Petaluma
Bicycle Factory
Boulevard
PETALUMA
Howard
Street
South
WALNUT PARK
Extension
Western Avenue
Street
Spring Hill Road
"D"
Road
Marin County Line
San Antonio Creek
Valley
Chileno
(Red Hill Road)
Wilson
Hill Road
CHEESE FACTORY

2 COTATI TO BLOOMFIELD

REGION: ***SOUTHERN SONOMA COUNTY***

MILEAGE: *24 MILES (4 - 5 HOURS RIDING TIME)*

RATING: *MEDIUM DIFFICULTY — A beautiful back road ride through the heart of the Sonoma farmlands. Very light traffic and good roads make this ride relatively easy; however, several moderate climbs and a long distance might make this trip more suitable to a well-conditioned rider. The trip should be planned for the morning, as strong headwinds come up in the afternoon and you may find yourself pedaling downhill!*

ROUTE: *From the Cotati Plaza, take West Sierra Avenue to Stony Point Road, turn left at Stony Point and right on Roblar Road to Valley Ford Road. Take Valley Ford Road to Bloomfield Road. Turn right to Bloomfield. Return to Valley Ford Road, turn left on Walker Road to Pepper Road, which leads right to Meecham Road and then becomes Stony Point Road. Turn right on West Sierra back to the plaza.*

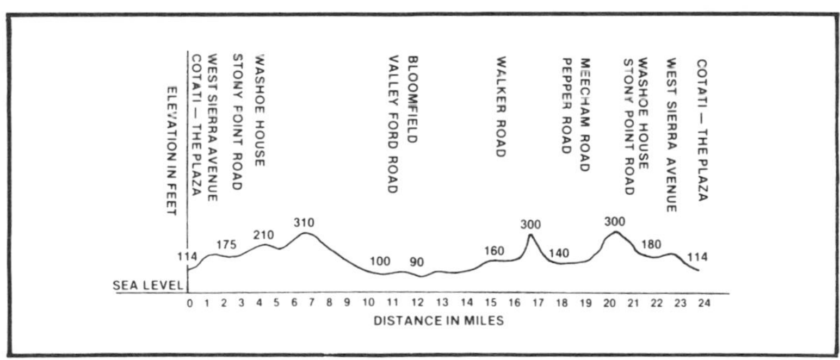

Begin your trip at the *Cotati Plaza,* a small and interesting place, with many of its local inhabitants being students from nearby Sonoma State University. Take West Sierra Avenue and follow it along until it passes under the freeway. This marks the entrance to the wide open country, complete with old chicken sheds, rolling farmlands and eucalyptus trees. At the stop sign turn left onto Stony Point Road. The road has a wide shoulder here for comfortable traveling. On your right you will see a breathtaking panoramic view of what I believe Sonoma County is famous for — its exquisitely rolling hills and tranquil dairy farms.

Washoe House is on your right, at the corner of Stony Point and Roblar Roads. It is the oldest roadhouse in California, built in 1859, and is still operating as a tavern and restaurant (a meal you may consider on the way back. I hear the food is superb.)

Take Roblar Road and view the scenery on your left. At Petersen Road you may want to take a side trip and tour *Petersen's Dairy*, or buy pumpkins or apples in the Fall. Backtrack to Roblar Road and continue on. At Valley Ford Road turn right and continue on until you reach Bloomfield Road. A sign on your left indicating *Stormy's Tavern* lets you know you've reached "downtown" *Bloomfield* (actually three streets and a fire house). On your left, before you reach Stormy's, is a wooden sign acknowledging *Emma Herbert Memorial Park*. Here you will find picnic tables, barbecue pit, and restrooms. If Stormy's is open you can pick up sandwiches, or just use the park for a quiet picnic lunch.

Return to Valley Ford Road and turn left. You will pass St. Anthony's Farms on your right, which is a church-operated dairy run by the Franciscan Fathers and part of Saint Anthony's Dining Room located in San Francisco. It offers temporary residence to 40 men until they are back on their feet again.

Turn left on Walker Road for a backroad ride to Pepper Road. Follow Pepper Road to Meecham Road and turn left. Meecham will bring you back to Stony Point Road. Turn left on Stony Point (now is the time to consider eating at the Washoe House) and then right on West Sierra, back to the Cotati Plaza and your car.

VARIATION: Instead of turning left on Walker Road, continue on Valley Ford Road where you will pass *Two Rock*, the location for the U.S. Coast Guard Training Center. Turn left on Pepper Road and continue the trip as described above.

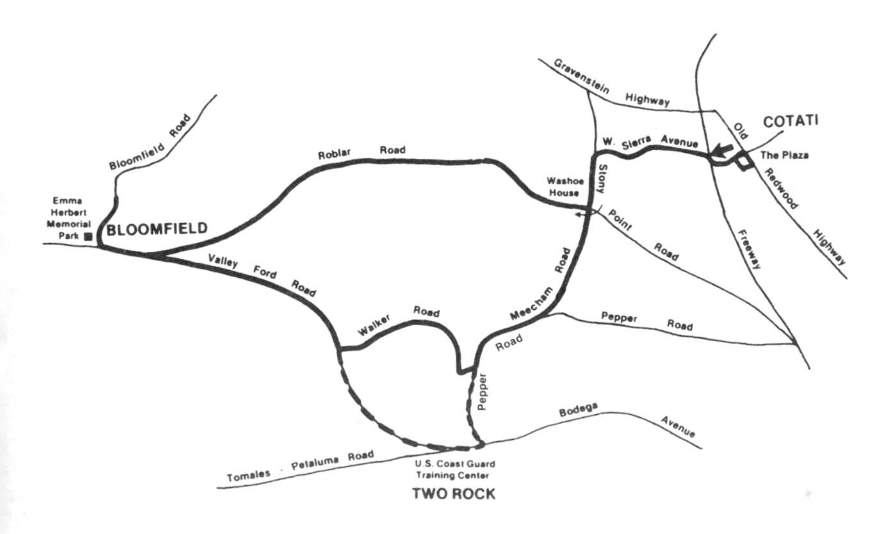

THE

3 PENNGROVE AREA LOOP TRIP

REGION: ***SOUTHERN SONOMA COUNTY***

MILEAGE: *10.5 MILES (1 HOUR RIDING TIME)*

RATING: *EASY RIDE — A short country ride through picturesque farmlands and gently rolling hills, with a timely pause for lunch or dinner. This is an excellent trip for a beginner or child (it was our first ride) because of its easy grades and short distance, yet it affords the experienced biker a chance to see what some of the Sonoma County back roads are all about.*

ROUTE: *From Penngrove Park go down Petaluma Hill Road, 1 mile; turn left at East Railroad Avenue, 4 miles, left at Stony Point Road and then right at Jewett Road. Jewett becomes Center Road, then Liberty Road. Turn left at Rainsville Road to Stony Point Road. Turn right to Old Redwood Highway. At Old Redwood Highway turn left and stay on that to Penngrove Park.*

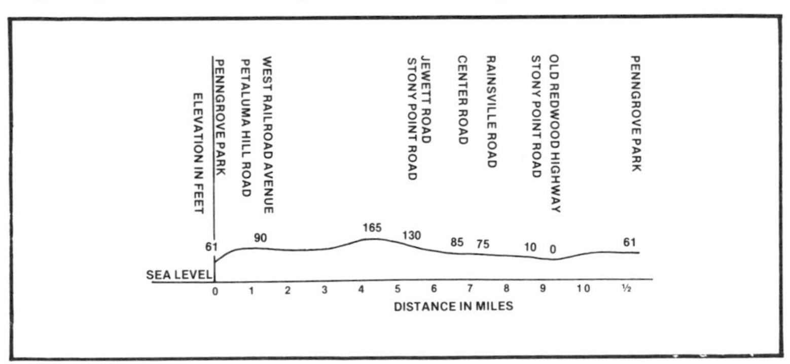

Begin the trip at Penngrove Park in *Penngrove*, a tiny rural community just 2 miles east of Highway 101. Penngrove was once a railroad stop, first named Penn, later Penn's Grove, and finally Penngrove. The new freeway has left Penngrove in rural peace and basically untouched.

Follow the main street, Petaluma Hill Road, through Penngrove and turn left on East Railroad Avenue. Here you will travel along peaceful country roads, passing homes with pigs, sheep, and cows in their backyards. The road will take you through attractive neighborhoods and then pass under the freeway, ending with an easy coast to Stony Point Road. Looking out from Stony Point Road is one of my favorite views — gently rolling hills, old dairies, numerous windmills that remind me of an age not yet forgotten.

Turn left on Stony Point for just a few feet and then right on Jewett Road.

Follow this winding road along scenic landscapes and tree-lined farms. Continue to Liberty Road and turn left at Rainsville Road. Enjoy a brisk coast for two or three miles until you stop again at Stony Point Road. Turn right on Stony Point to Old Redwood Highway. There will be heavy traffic after this point, as it has become more developed. So be careful.

The intersection of Stony Point Road and Old Redwood Highway offers the hungry biker a chance to grab a sandwich, dessert or a full-course meal from the numerous restaurants on either side of the freeway.

Complete your trip along Old Redwood Highway, back to Penngrove. If there is room in your pack (or in your tummy) be sure to stop at *Palace of Fruit* for an excellent selection of fresh fruits and vegetables. If you wish to stop for a picnic lunch, you can eat under shade trees of *Penngrove Park.*

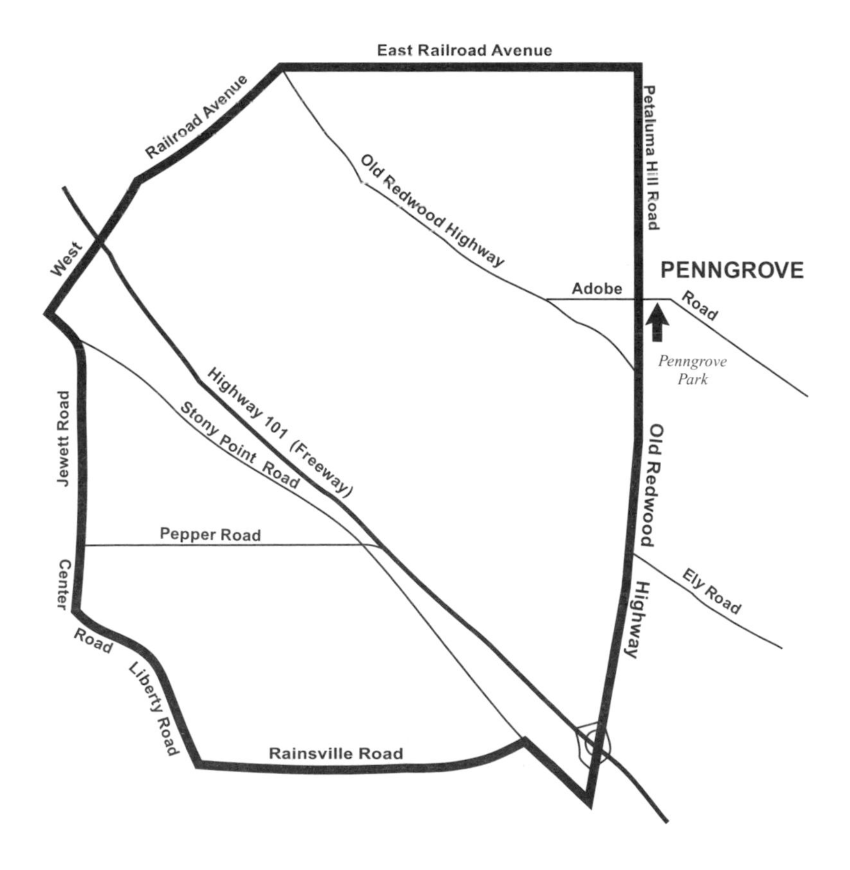

II. THE SONOMA VALLEY *"Valley of the Moon"*

I would rather be ashes than dust!
I would rather that my spark should burn out in a brilliant blaze than it should be stifled by dryrot.

I would rather be a superb meteor, every atom of me in magnificent glow, than a sleepy and permanent planet.

The proper function of man is to live, not to exist.

I shall not waste my days in trying to prolong them. I shall use my time.

JACK LONDON

"Wolf House"

4 CITY OF SONOMA HISTORIC RAMBLE

REGION: ***THE SONOMA VALLEY "Valley of the Moon"***

MILEAGE: *11 MILES (1-1½ HOURS RIDING TIME)*

RATING: *VERY EASY RIDE — Spend an entire day touring historic Sonoma, using your bicycle to take you back to the days of ear/y California. A fun and educational trip for the whole family.*

The first part of this tour begins at the *Sonoma Plaza,* the largest and most interesting of its kind in California. It is the site of many festivals, parades, and historical events. The Plaza's, and Sonoma's uniqueness is that the old (for some lucky reason) was never swept away. On the north end of the Plaza you will observe building after building dating back before California became part of the United States. Some of the buildings are private or commercial, such as the *Salvador Vallejo Home,* the *Swiss Hotel* and the *Blue Wing Inn.*

The Plaza's also a pleasant place for a picnic when your tour is over. It has grassy lawns, duck ponds, and play areas for the kids. *The Sonoma Cheese Factory* offers local wines and other deli goodies.

The best way to explore the plaza is to park your car on the Plaza or in the Public Parking lot off First Street East. Leave your bikes on your car and walk casually around, checking out the quaint shops and historic buildings, most of which are situated at the north end of the Plaza.

"CASA GRANDE," built in 1836, was the first adobe home of General Vallejo while Sonoma was a Mexican town. It was later destroyed by fire in 1867. Only the Indian servants' wing remains. Entire families lived in each room.

TOSCANO HOTEL, next door, was first built as a general store and library in 1850's and then converted to a hotel in 1886. View life as it was lived 100 years ago, complete with furniture of the period.

SONOMA BARRACKS, built of redwood timbers and adobe brick in 1835 by General Vallejo, was used to house Mexican army troops. In 1846 it became the headquarters of the Bear Flag Party.

MISSION SAN FRANCISCO SOLANO DE SONOMA, last and northernmost of California's 21 missions, was built in 1823, and has been completely restored. The mission was a religious and cultural center and today houses an outstanding collection of California historical artifacts and antiques.

BLUE WING INN, across from the Mission, was built in 1840 and was one of the oldest hotels in northern California. Now it houses antique and craft shops. *El Paso de Sonoma,* a complex of small craft stores and shops is in the style of a Mexican courtyard.

BEAR FLAG MONUMENT, standing in the northeast corner of the Plaza, celebrates 25 turbulent days in 1846 when Sonoma became the capital of the Republic of California. On June 14th, American horsemen raised the original Bear Flag, which became the first state flag and led to American rule throughout California.

Now is the time to grab your bikes and start riding. Take E. Spain Street past the Mission until you reach 4th Street. Here you will see that the charm of Sonoma extends well past its tourist-oriented plaza and curio shops. Dozens of turn-of-the-century houses — small, unpretentious and neat — surround you, bearing witness to the town's well kept and well-planned age. You might wonder if the street has changed at all in the last 70 years.

A left turn on 4th Street brings you to *Sebastiani Vineyards* — the location of the first vineyard planted north of San Francisco. It was first used by the mission fathers for production of sacramental wines. You can tour the mellow old stone building and investigate their well-supplied wine-tasting room. Notice the bas-relief wood carvings on the casks, doors, and walls of the winery which were done by 77-year old Earl Brown.

From *Sebastiani,* pedal south on 4th Street to Napa Street, turn left and follow signs to *Buena Vista Winery* another legendary winery. Take a self-conducted tour through Buena Vista's aging cellars and wine-tasting room, built in cool limestone caverns where the temperature remains a constant 45°F. Here America's first big experimental vineyard was established in 1862 by a Hungarian nobleman, Count Agoston Haraszthy. Shaded picnic tables are placed strategically around the grounds to help you enjoy your lunch, along with a bottle of one of Buena Vista's delicious wines.

From *Buena Vista* return to Napa Street, turn right, then right again on 7th Street and follow signs to *Bartholomew Park Winery.* The road is rather bumpy, but it takes you past attractive tree-lined vineyards and elegant homes. The first fine European wine grapes grown in America were planted here in 1862. There is a hospitality room and picnic area, and a beautiful wine garden which overlooks a duck pond shaded by large oak trees.

From *Bartholomew* go straight down 7th Street, 1½ miles, to Denmark Street. Turn right on Denmark and then left on 5th Street. At Napa Road turn right to Broadway and turn right again to *Train Town.*

Train Town, a 10-acre railroad park, is the home of the Sonoma Gaslight Western Railroad, a scale reproduction of the 1890 period. Here you can take a 15-minute train ride behind a steam-powered locomotive.

From Train Town return to Napa Road (which becomes Leveroni Road) and turn right ½-mile to Fifth Street (just before the bridge). Turn right on Fifth, 1 mile, until you reach West Spain Street. Go half a block further to the bike path. Turn right on the bike path, which will take you right to *Vallejo's Home.*

"LACHRYMA MONTIS," "Tear of the Mountain," so named because a large spring is on the site, is the Victorian home of General Vallejo, and was built in 1851. Visitors may tour both the home and storage house, which are now state museums.

Follow the bike path back to the plaza and your car. You have had a full day!

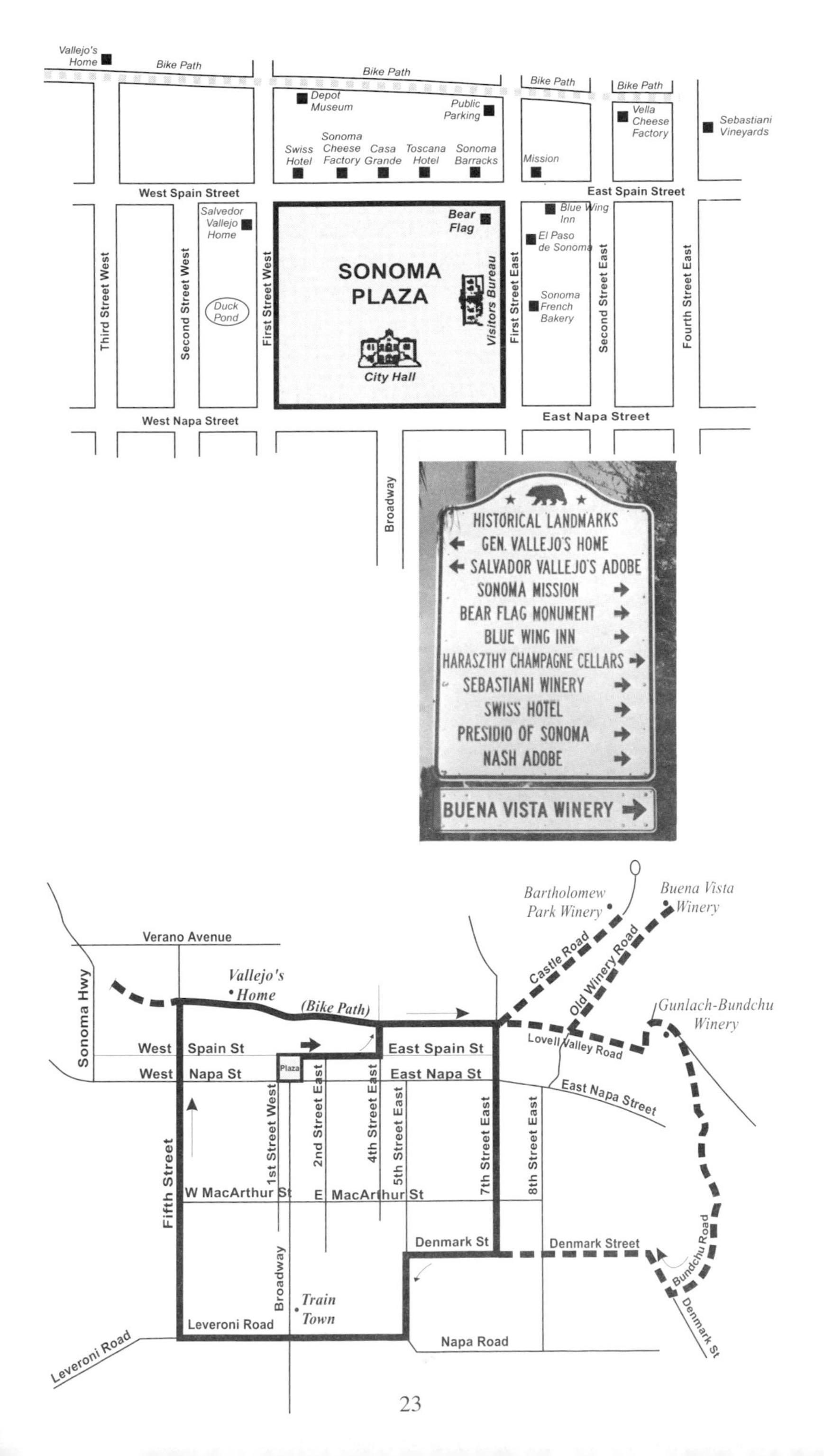
Vallejo's Home
Bike Path
Bike Path
Bike Path
Bike Path
Depot Museum
Public Parking
Vella Cheese Factory
Sebastiani Vineyards
Sonoma Cheese Factory
Swiss Hotel
Casa Grande
Toscana Hotel
Sonoma Barracks
Mission
West Spain Street
East Spain Street
Salvedor Vallejo Home
Bear Flag
Blue Wing Inn
El Paso de Sonoma
SONOMA PLAZA
Visitors Bureau
Sonoma French Bakery
Third Street West
Second Street West
Duck Pond
First Street West
First Street East
Second Street East
Fourth Street East
City Hall
West Napa Street
East Napa Street
Broadway
HISTORICAL LANDMARKS
GEN. VALLEJO'S HOME
SALVADOR VALLEJO'S ADOBE
SONOMA MISSION
BEAR FLAG MONUMENT
BLUE WING INN
HARASZTHY CHAMPAGNE CELLARS
SEBASTIANI WINERY
SWISS HOTEL
PRESIDIO OF SONOMA
NASH ADOBE
BUENA VISTA WINERY
Bartholomew Park Winery
Buena Vista Winery
Verano Avenue
Castle Road
Old Winery Road
Sonoma Hwy
Vallejo's Home
(Bike Path)
Gunlach-Bundchu Winery
West Spain St
East Spain St
Lovell Valley Road
West Napa St
Plaza
East Napa St
East Napa Street
1st Street West
2nd Street East
4th Street East
5th Street East
7th Street East
8th Street East
Fifth Street
W MacArthur St
E MacArthur St
Denmark St
Denmark Street
Bundchu Road
Broadway
Train Town
Leveroni Road
Leveroni Road
Napa Road
Denmark St

5 SONOMA TO GLEN ELLEN

REGION: ***THE SONOMA VALLEY "Valley of the Moon"***

MILEAGE: *16 MILES (2-3 HOURS RIDING TIME)*
19 MILES, INCLUDING JACK LONDON STATE PARK (3-4 HOURS RIDING TIME)

RATING: *MEDIUM DIFFICULTY TO GLEN ELLEN (CHALLENGING, IF YOU ADD JACK LONDON STATE PARK) The route to Glen Ellen is a relatively easy one, few hills and very scenic — a good trip for the whole family. The road to Jack London State Park is a 400-foot climb in 1½ miles. In other words, prepare to be pooped.*

ROUTE: *From the Sonoma Plaza, take West Napa Street to Sonoma Highway (Highway 12); turn right. Turn left on Madrone Road to Arnold Drive. Turn right on Arnold Drive and continue until you reach Glen Ellen. If desired, follow signs to Jack London State Park. Return on Arnold Drive.*

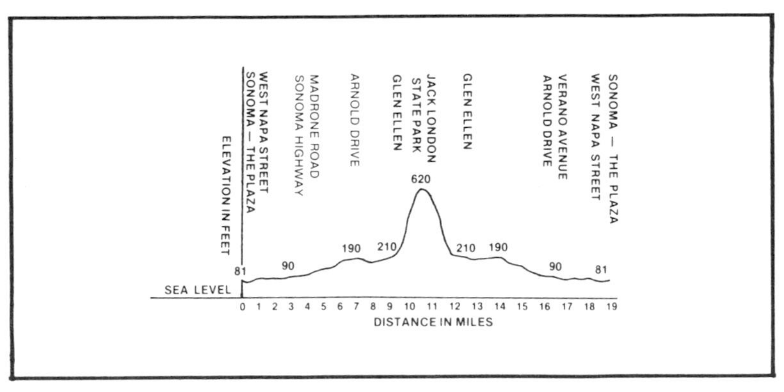

Note: This route has been changed because of the increasingly dangerous conditions along parts of Arnold Drive. At this time Sonoma Highway appears to be the safest route for getting to Glen Ellen. Arnold Drive, however, is more preferable for the trip back to Sonoma.

Begin the trip at the Sonoma Plaza. Find West Napa Street and turn right. Napa is a busy street, with fast-moving traffic, but you will not stay on it for more than a few blocks. Turn right on Sonoma Highway, which is also a busy street with fast-moving traffic, but it is also wide enough to be fairly safe and it also has a good bike lane.

Turn left on Madrone Road, then right on Arnold Drive, a scenic road with tree-lined homes and a lovely panorama of the hills on your right. There are broad shoulders with little traffic. You will pedal through the pleasant landscaped grounds of Sonoma State Hospital and pass over a bridge to find *London Glen Village*, a complex of boutiques and craft galleries built into an old winery. It's an interesting place to browse. For you Jack London fans, the *Jack London Bookstore*, across the road, has most of Jack London's books as well as other London memorabilia.

However you approach *Glen Ellen*, it appears rather suddenly. It hides in trees, quite literally a glen, with creeks and homes nestled in the hills. Now is the time for you to make a decision. The steep 1½-mile (the sign is inaccurate) ride up to *Jack London State Park* will poop out even the experienced biker, but you'll appreciate the lush landscaping as you walk your bike up the steeper grades. At the park, you can see the "House of Happy Walls" museum. You can walk through the quiet countryside to London's grave and view the great stone mansion, *Wolf House,* that burned down. If you've never been there it is well worth seeing. It's a pleasant place to have a picnic and relax after your trip, and you can view London's *Valley of the Moon* as well. From the park, enjoy a thrilling coast back down to Glen Ellen. Whether or not you decide to see the park, you will be returning to Sonoma via Arnold Drive.

VARIATION #1: Extend your trip 13 miles by riding through Glen Ellen and then turning left on Warm Springs Road, which is forested and shady. At the junction of Warm Springs and Sonoma Mountain Roads, turn right to stay on Warm Springs Road. You might consider going to *Morton's* for a refreshing swim in one of their pools, returning back to Bennett Valley Road. If not, turn left at Bennett Valley Road and continue your trip. At Enterprise Road, take a sharp left and coast most of the way back down to Sonoma Mountain Road. Turn left at Sonoma Mountain Road back to Glen Ellen. This back road ride has a beautiful country atmosphere through winding brush forest with no traffic to interfere with your viewing. Return to Sonoma on Arnold Drive.

VARIATION #2: When you get back to Sonoma you might want to take the *City of Sonoma Historic Ramble*, if you have energy to spare. It will add 11 miles to your trip and allow you to do some fantastic sightseeing as well.

VARIATION #3: Combine your trip with *Glen Ellen to Kenwood* by turning left on Warm Springs Road and returning on Sonoma Highway and then on Dunbar Road. This will extend your trip 10½ miles.

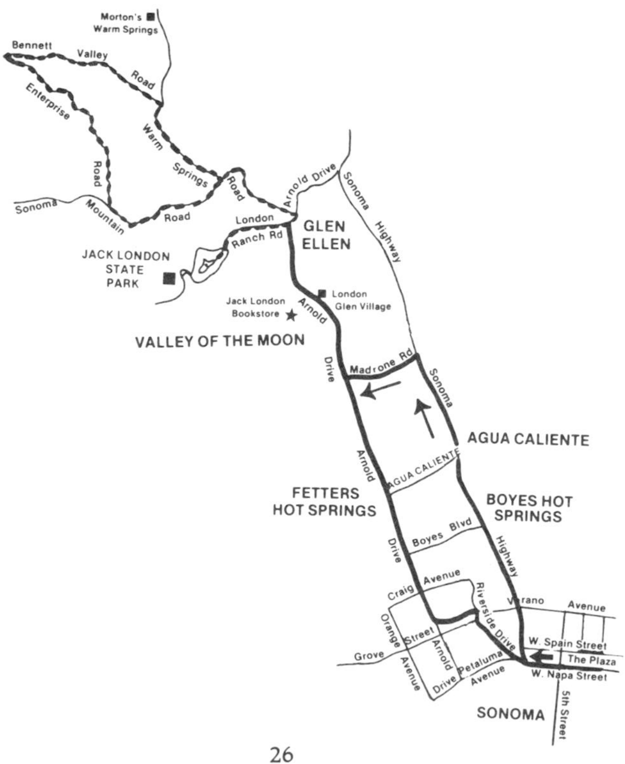
Morton's Warm Springs
Bennett Valley Road
Enterprise Road
Warm Springs Road
Sonoma Mountain Road
London Ranch Rd
Arnold Drive
Sonoma Highway
GLEN ELLEN
JACK LONDON STATE PARK
London Glen Village
Jack London Bookstore
VALLEY OF THE MOON
Madrone Rd
AGUA CALIENTE
FETTERS HOT SPRINGS
BOYES HOT SPRINGS
Boyes Blvd
Craig Avenue
Riverside Drive
Verano Avenue
Orange Avenue
Street
Grove
Petaluma Avenue
W. Spain Street
The Plaza
W. Napa Street
5th Street
SONOMA

6 GLEN ELLEN TO KENWOOD

REGION: ***THE SONOMA VALLEY "Valley of the Moon"***

MILEAGE: *10.5 MILES (1 - 2 HOURS RIDING TIME)*

RATING: *EASY RIDE — A flat scenic tour through the Sonoma Valley on picturesque wooded back roads. A trip that the whole family can enjoy.*

ROUTE: *Begin at Glen Ellen. Take Arnold Drive through town and turn left at Warm Springs Road. Follow it to Kenwood, 3 miles. Turn right on Sonoma Highway, and right on to Dunbar Road, which leads into Arnold Drive and brings you back to Glen Ellen.*

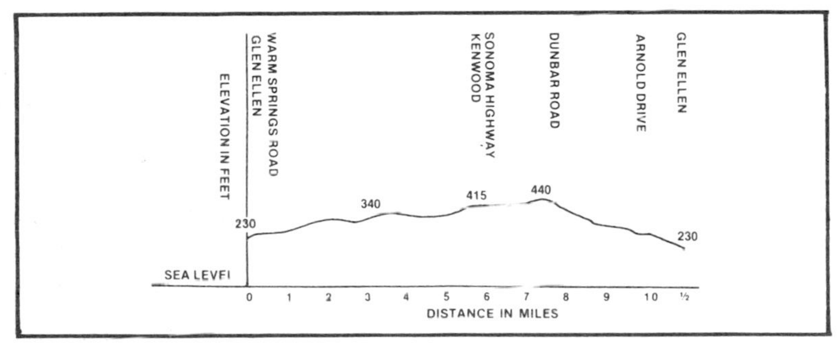

Begin your trip in the heart of *Glen Ellen*, Jack London's famous town. Ride through town and turn left onto Warm Springs Road. Few cars use this road and you will be immediately transported from the feeling of town to one of tranquil forest. The road gets rather winding and narrow, but the absence of cars will more than compensate.

At each fork in the road, bear to the right and the road will take you directly to *Kenwood*, a small town with a cluster of rather attractive stores that line Sonoma Highway. Across the road is the *Kenwood Winery*, which is a good place to sample the local wines. Further north on Sonoma Highway is another winery, *Chateau St. Jean*, that you may also be interested in visiting.

Turn right onto Sonoma Highway and follow it for 2½ miles. This part of the trip is smooth with fairly wide shoulders, but there is steady traffic, so you must be careful to stay as close to the side of the road as possible. The billboard "Sebastiani Winery" brings you to Dunbar Road, which is a narrow country road, lined with vineyards and all sorts of trees and is quite peaceful compared to the bustle of the highway. Take Dunbar Road for another 2 miles until it becomes Arnold Drive. This road, wide and smooth, leads you right back to Glen Ellen.

VARIATION #1: If you still have energy to expend you might consider visiting *Jack London State Historic Park.* It is a 400-foot climb of 1½ miles, but the view of the *Valley of the Moon* is excellent and the museum is interesting.

VARIATION #2: You might wish to coordinate this trip with the *Sonoma to Glen Ellen* trip by continuing past Glen Ellen on Arnold Drive until you reach Sonoma. Return on Arnold Drive. This will add another 16 miles to your trip.

VARIATION #3: For the super bike enthusiast, you might wish to continue on to Ithaca, New York, as the sign indicates — *only 2,873 miles!*

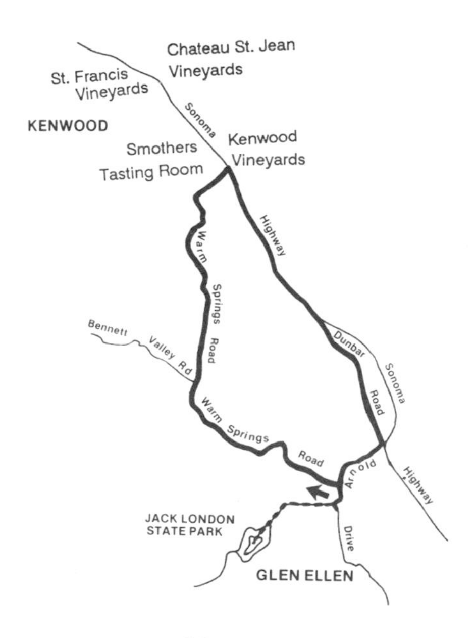

Chateau St. Jean
Vineyards
St. Francis
Vineyards
KENWOOD
Sonoma
Smothers
Tasting Room
Kenwood
Vineyards
Highway
Warm
Springs
Road
Bennett
Valley Rd
Dunbar
Road
Sonoma
Warm
Springs
Road
Arnold
Highway
JACK LONDON
STATE PARK
Drive
GLEN ELLEN

III. NORTHERN SONOMA COUNTY

GRAPES

I shall not miss the roses, fading
As soon as spring's fleet days are done;
I like the grapes whose clusters ripen
Upon the hillside in the sun —
The glory of my fertile valley,
They hang, each lustrous as a pearl,
Gold autumn's joy: oblong, transparent,
Like the slim fingers of a girl.

ALEXANDER PUSHKIN

7 HEALDSBURG DRY CREEK VALLEY

REGION: ***NORTHERN SONOMA COUNTY***

MILEAGE: *12 MILES (2-3 HOURS RIDING TIME)*

RATING: *MEDIUM DIFFICULTY — A narrow, rural valley, surrounded by lush hillsides winding through a sea of private vineyards. Easy grades and a scenic landscape make this a very pleasant trip.*

ROUTE: *From the plaza, take Healdsburg Avenue to Dry Creek Road. Turn left at Lambert Bridge Road and left again at West Dry Creek Road. Turn left at Westside Road back to the Plaza.*

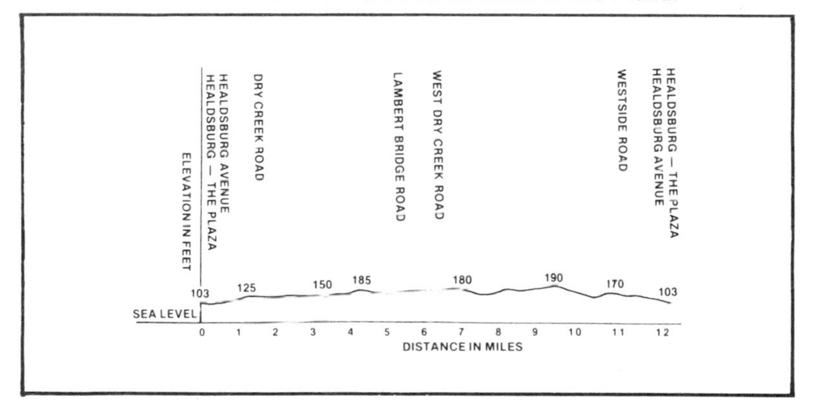

Begin your trip at the *Healdsburg Plaza.* Take Healdsburg Avenue north and turn left at Dry Creek Road. You will initially encounter gently rolling hills with moderate traffic until you reach a small market, *Dry Creek General Store,* at the corner of Dry Creek and Lambert Bridge Roads. This is an excellent place to stop for a brief rest on their veranda with country benches. Fill your pack with an extra snack or lunch, since they also have a small deli.

Turn up Lambert Bridge Road and be sure to stop at *Dry Creek Vineyards.* This small, friendly winery is a family operation. We always enjoy stopping here and tasting their current selection of wines, and often find ourselves returning at the end of the trip to make a purchase. They are open daily and picnic facilities are available.

From the winery, the road winds down and crosses Dry Creek at Lambert Bridge. Here the creek is quite scenic in contrast to the view closer to Healdsburg where gravel is currently being excavated.

Turn left when you reach West Dry Creek Road and you will find yourself on a quiet country road. Very few cars pass along here and the road is shaded by the hillside and accented with numerous orchards. On the left you will enjoy an impressive panoramic view of Geyser Peak, Cobb Mountain, and Mount St. Helena. West Dry Creek Road ends at Westside Road and you can complete this loop by turning left and riding into the "bustling" town of *Healdsburg*. There are several small cafes and restaurants you can go to for lunch, or you can picnic under the shade trees of the plaza.

Healdsburg is a charming old town with an active commercial district surrounding a central plaza. During the summer you may stop at *Healdsburg Memorial Beach* for a swim in the Russian River. Facilities include bath houses, picnic-barbecue park, and a refreshment stand. The area is especially beautiful in March when prune trees are in blossom. Healdsburg is becoming the fastest growing vintage-producing area in California.

VARIATION #1: For an extended trip, continue up Dry Creek Road to Yoakim Bridge Road, cross Dry Creek and return south on West Dry Creek Road, meeting up with the shorter trip at Lambert Bridge Road.

VARIATION #2: Continue on Dry Creek Road, past Yoakim Bridge Road until you reach Warm Springs Dam. There you can take a tour of the Fish Hatchery and follow the road to the Overlook. This will give you a breathtaking view of Lake Sonoma and an expanse of the Sonoma County valley.

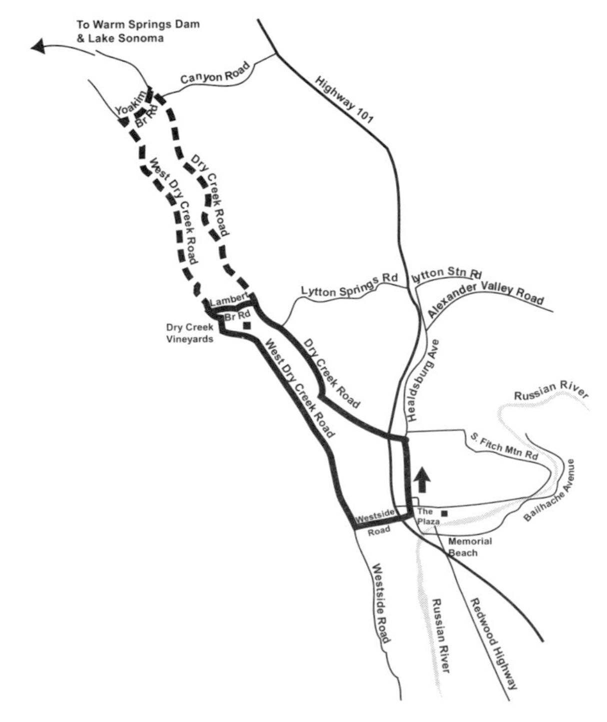

8 GEYSERVILLE ALEXANDER VALLEY WINE TOUR

REGION: *NORTHERN SONOMA COUNTY*

MILEAGE: *21.5 MILES (3 - 4 HOURS RIDING TIME)*

RATING: *MEDIUM DIFFICULTY — A colorful ride over relatively flat terrain, passing many interesting wineries and other attractive places to stop.*

ROUTE: *Begin in the center of Geyserville and turn left onto State Highway 128. Follow it as it turns right and then right again onto Alexander Valley Road. Turn right on Lytton Station Road and right again onto Lytton Springs Road. Go under the freeway and turn right on Dry Creek Road and right on Canyon Road. This will bring you back to Geyserville Avenue; turn right here to Geyserville and your car.*

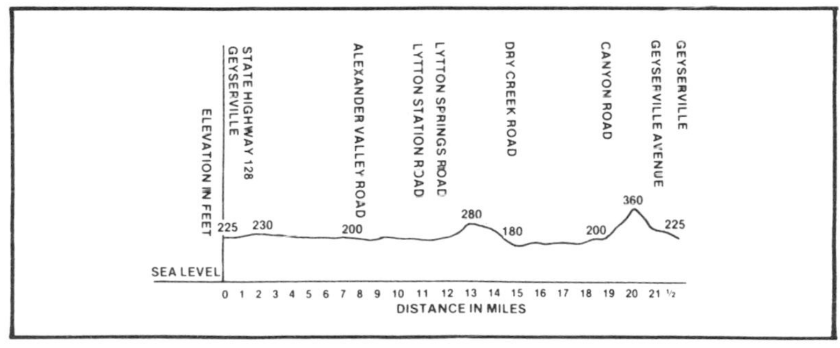

Begin your ride in the center of *Geyserville,* called "The Gateway to the Geysers." It takes its name from the steam geysers just a few miles to the east. Take State Highway 128 east, which is perpendicular to Geyserville Avenue. The road is flat and there are few cars. You will turn right and continue along the foothills. On the right you can see an expanse of vineyards. On the left looms Sulphur Peak, which provides comfortable shade for your ride (if you ride in the morning).

You will reach a junction where the sign tells you that *The Geysers* are only 16 miles away, a place where steam from the earth has been captured and is used to produce enough power for the needs of nearly one million people. This might be a good extension for your trip. From what I have heard, though, the road is quite steep — The Geysers are at a 2,000-foot elevation — so you decide for yourself. If not, turn right and follow the highway instead. Here the road becomes wide and smooth. You will pass vineyards all through this trip looking out over the valley. Turn right at Alexander Valley Road — the sign tells you that Healdsburg is 6 miles away. You will cross over the Russian River, a nice place to stop for a picnic or a swim before continuing on.

For those of you who wish to stay in the area for a day or so, *Alexander Valley Campground* is a nice place to stop. Continue on and turn right at Lytton Station Road. The road gets rough and narrow, the countryside becomes more barren. At the stop sign turn right onto Lytton Springs Road and continue under the freeway. Here you enter a forested area providing welcome relief on a hot day. You will pass the Salvation Army Center and begin encountering some rolling hills. Healdsburg Airport is on your left. The road narrows, but there is no traffic.

Turn right onto Dry Creek Road. The road widens to provide a good bike path and, of course, more traffic. (It seems you can't have one without the other.) Make a right on Canyon Road. This is the only really large grade you will be encountering. You will pass *Pedroncelli Winery* and later on *Geyser Peak Winery.* Both are interesting stops for sampling good local wines.

Continue on and ride under the freeway. Turn right on Geyserville Avenue, which will take you back to the heart of Geyserville and your car.

VARIATION: You might wish to take a short detour by turning left on Red Winery Road for a panoramic view of the Alexander Valley.

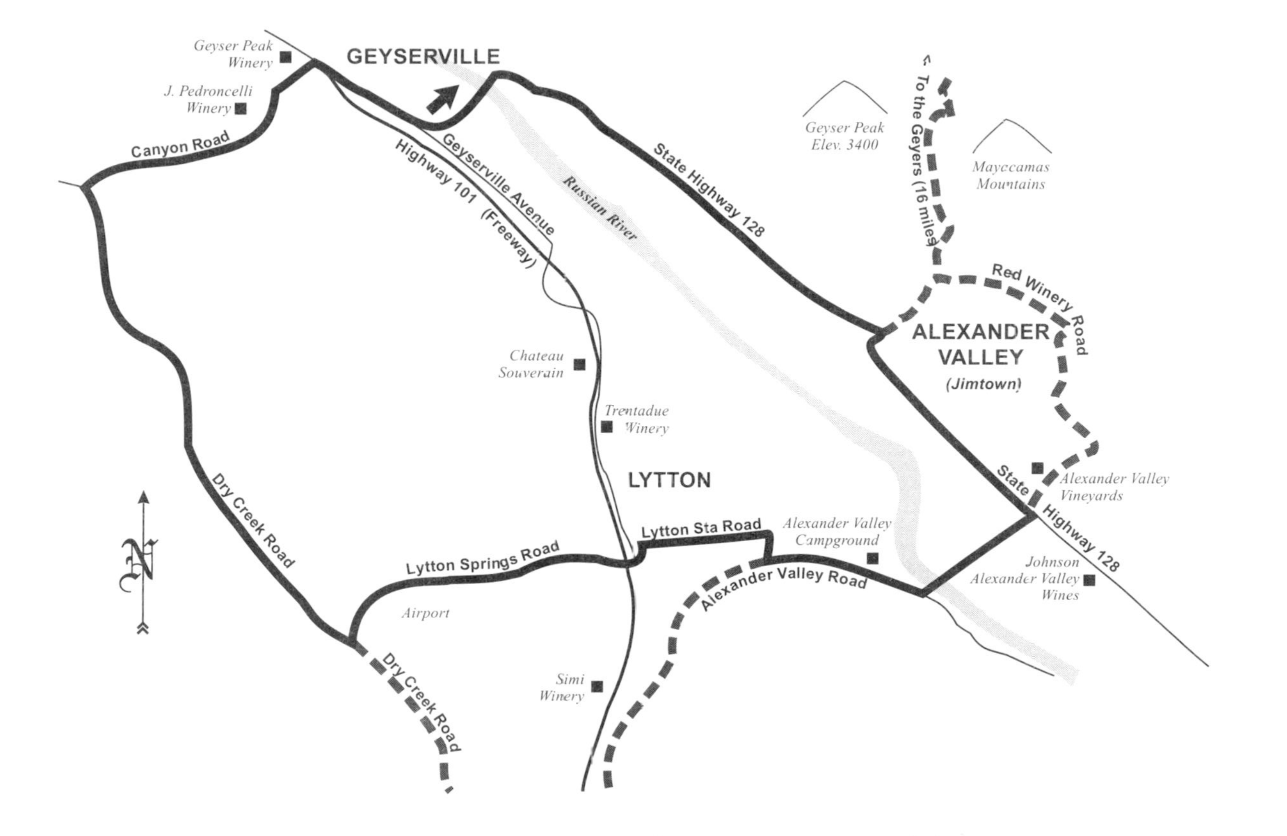

GEYSERVILLE
Geyser Peak Winery
J. Pedroncelli Winery
Canyon Road
Geyserville Avenue
Highway 101 (Freeway)
Russian River
State Highway 128
Geyser Peak Elev. 3400
To the Geyers (16 miles)
Mayccamas Mountains
Red Winery Road
ALEXANDER VALLEY
(Jimtown)
Chateau Souverain
Trentadue Winery
LYTTON
State Highway 128
Alexander Valley Vineyards
Lytton Sta Road
Alexander Valley Campground
Johnson Alexander Valley Wines
Lytton Springs Road
Alexander Valley Road
Dry Creek Road
Airport
Simi Winery
Dry Creek Road

9 CLOVERDALE TO ASTI

REGION: NORTHERN SONOMA COUNTY

MILEAGE: *11½ MILES (2-3 HOURS RIDING TIME)*

RATING: *EASY — A relatively flat ride that passes through lush vineyards and winds around the foothills and rolling countryside. This ride may not be possible during the rainy winter months because the Asti Bridge may be closed.*

ROUTE: *Begin on First Street in Cloverdale, which becomes Crocker Road; turn right onto River Road for about 5 miles which turns onto Washington School Road (no signs to indicate this). Turn right at Asti Road which will return you to Cloverdale and First Street.*

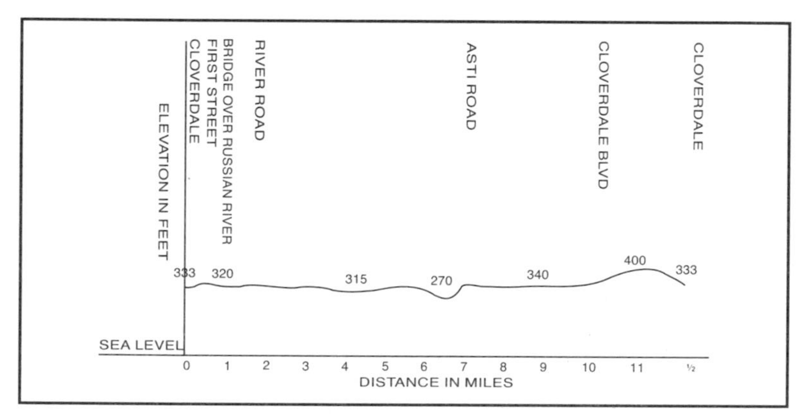

Begin your trip on Cloverdale Boulevard in downtown Cloverdale, Sonoma County's northernmost town. Its attractions include many festivals and activities throughout the year, including the annual Citrus Fair in February. Nearby are two unique churches modeled after wine vats. Cloverdale is also the northernmost spot in the United States where oranges and lemons are grown commercially.

Turn right on First Street. The road is wide with little traffic. It becomes Crocker Road and you will shortly cross a bridge over the Russian River. This may be a good place to stop and take a splash if the weather is hot. There will be another spot further along if this is too early in your ride. Crocker Road turns sharply right onto River Road. This winding road exposes the foothills on the left and lush vineyards on the right. There is no bike path here, but the road is smooth with little traffic. There are hardly any grades, so relax and have a good time.

Further up a bit the road roughens and narrows as it approaches the second bridge across the Russian River. This is a good midway spot to swim and enjoy a picnic lunch. You will notice canoes passing here and local people who bring their rubber rafts. Summertime is lazy in these parts and great for splashing in the river on a hot day.

Continue your ride by turning right onto Asti Road, following it until it returns to the town of Cloverdale at First Street. Turn left and return to South Cloverdale Blvd. As an alternative, you can turn left at Theresa Drive (which goes under the freeway), then turn right onto Dutcher Creek Road, which becomes South Cloverdale Blvd., leading you back into town.

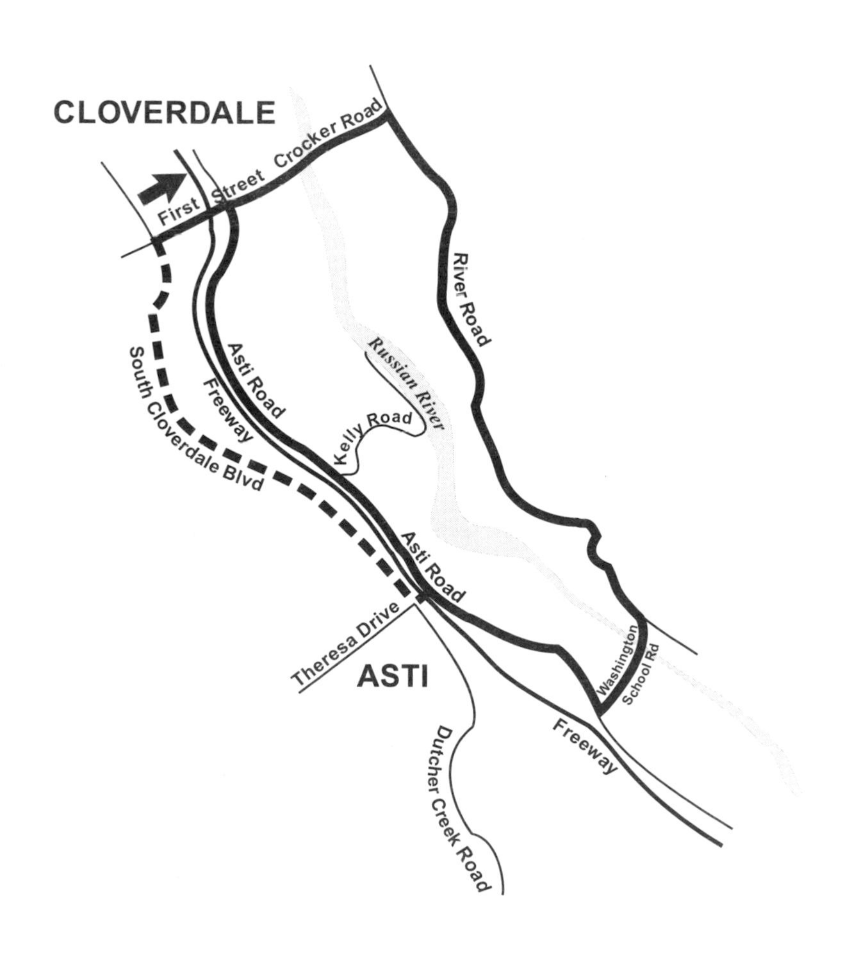

Russian River from bridge over Crocker Road in Cloverdale Photo: Rawls Frazier

Olive trees on Asti Road near Washington School Road Photo: Rawls Frazier

IV. THE RUSSIAN RIVER REGION

REDWOODS

Older than Age itself
they stand
And I sit silent in their shade,
surrounded by these tender giants.
They have no match on earth
yet still they strive
Pushing upward, ever upward
against the sky.
With an awe that feels like loneliness
though never quite alone —
For here, only here, is the sense
of all the Universe come to
make its spirit known.

MARYLYNNE SLAYEN

10 GUERNEVILLE TO ARMSTRONG WOODS

REGION: ***THE RUSSIAN RIVER REGION***

MILEAGE: *6½ MILES (1 HOUR RIDING TIME)*

RATING: *EASY RIDE – A scenic tour through the splendor and majesty of the famous California redwoods. The road to the park is wide and flat, ideal for beginning bicyclists and children. This is a great way to enjoy the Russian River Region and still have lots of time for other diversions in Guerneville, the playground of the area.*

ROUTE: *Armstrong Woods Road, 2 miles, to the State Park. A tour through the park, another 2 miles, and back to Guerneville.*

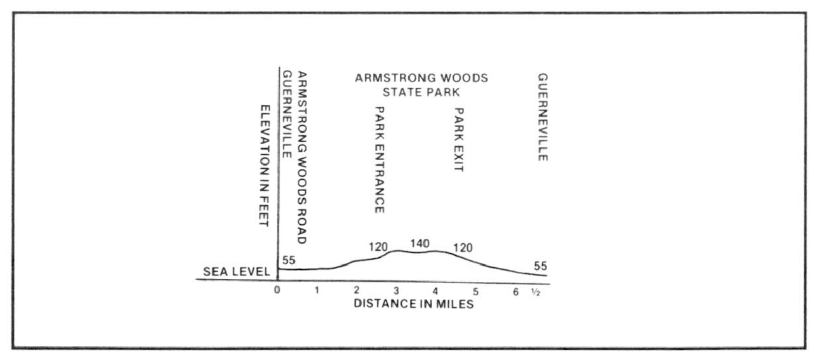

Guerneville, formerly called "Stumptown," was once prime redwood country. The redwoods around Guerneville were one of the grandest ever seen. Only small stands remain, such as in Armstrong Woods. The town was renamed Guerneville (Gurnville) in honor of George Emile Guerne, an enterprising Swiss who came looking for gold and ended up cutting trees instead. *Stumptown Days* is still a favorite event in June. In its honor Guerneville holds a town parade.

Resort life began here in the 1870's and flourished as vacationers came to see the wonders of the giant trees and discovered the beauty of the Russian River. Swimming, boating and water sports are popular in the summer; hiking and picnicking are big in the spring and fall; and fishermen flock here in winter when the steelhead are running. Biking naturally, is great here in any season.

From the bustle of Guerneville, follow the road that says Armstrong Woods Road. This will bring you right to the entrance of the park. The road leading there is wide and flat and has lots of room for bicycles. You will pass camping areas and several interesting shops along the way.

Armstrong Redwoods State Park contains 400 acres of natural forest growth, several picnic areas with barbecue pits, and marked hiking trails. The Forest Theater, a natural amphitheater, has a seating capacity for over 2,000 people and is often the setting for outdoor concerts (Sundays in July and August) ballet, church services and weddings. The Colonel Armstrong Tree is over 1,400 years old and climbs to 308 feet!

Bicycles are permitted in the park without fee, whereas cars have to pay. Follow the paved and shaded road through the forest. Explore the many different paths. Spend a glorious day picnicking in the cool forest, or sitting peacefully under the giant redwoods before returning back to Guerneville — and civilization. It's really a treat.

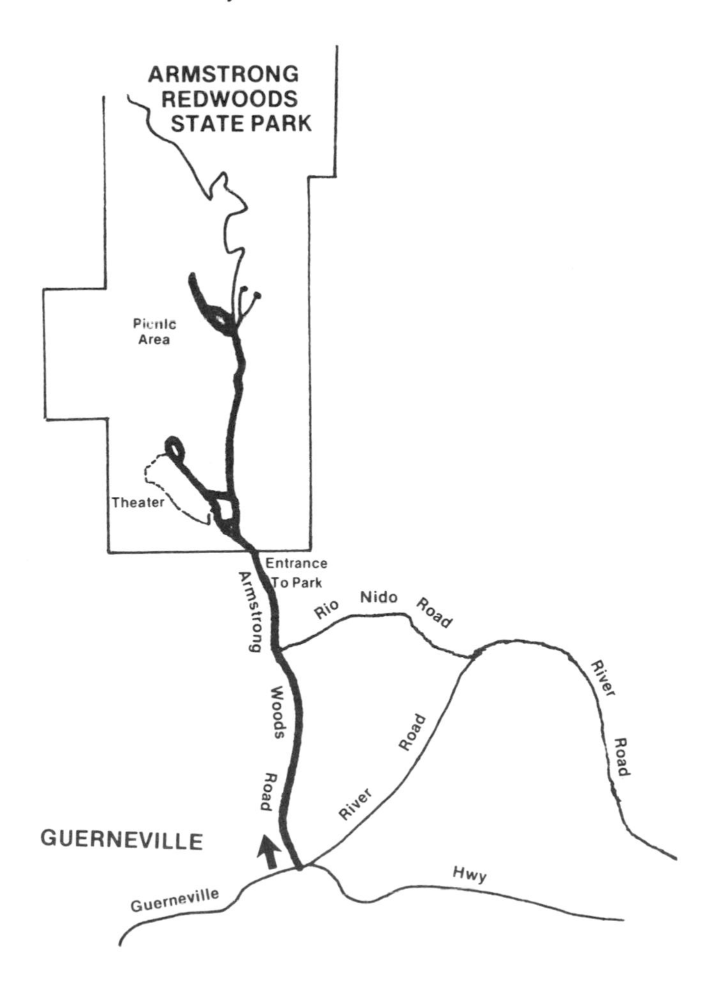

11 GUERNEVILLE River Road Ride

REGION: *THE RUSSIAN RIVER REGION*

MILEAGE: *19½ MILES (2-3 HOURS RIDING TIME)*

RATING: *MEDIUM DIFFICULTY — An easy, relatively flat tour of the wooded River Road area, punctuated with cool, forested roads and vast miles of incredible vineyards. Because of the length of the ride it can be considered to be moderately difficult for some beginners or out-of-condition riders.*

ROUTE: *Take River Road 7 miles. After crossing the bridge turn right onto Old River Road. Turn left at Wohler Road, 3 miles, cross the bridge and turn left onto Westside Road, 4 miles, which rejoins River Road. Take that back to Guerneville.*

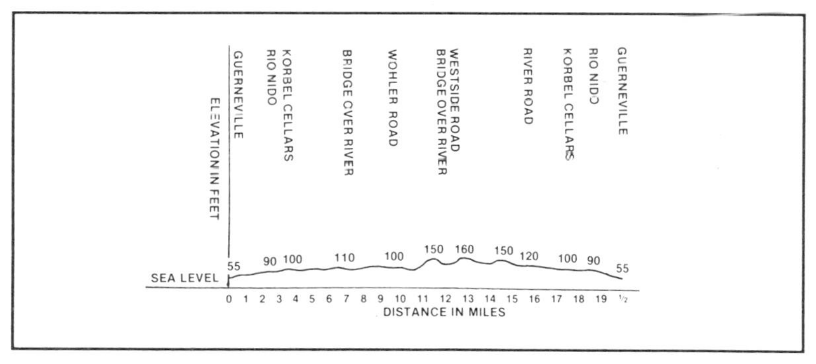

Begin your trip in the heart of Guerneville and take River Road towards Rio Nido. There is moderate traffic here but the road is easy to travel on. You will pass through the small but charming town of *Rio Nido,* the town "where memories linger." Just past Rio Nido, River Road suddenly illuminates a giddy expanse of vineyards and breathtaking hills. The mid-summer smells of blackberries and anise make you feel rich and alive. The road is flat and the going is easy, so this is a good time to enjoy the sights and aromas around you.

Shortly you will see signs beckoning you to *Korbel Cellars,* a winery famous for its champagne, made in the old, traditional style of winemaking. Tours that take you through the cellars and give you a step-by-step description of how wine is made are conducted every 45 minutes. A large, elegant tasting room offers you a selection of Korbel's finest wines. You will be passing by Korbel on the return trip and may find it more enjoyable then. Either time will be a treat.

River Road continues to be flat, but now becomes more forested, filled with tourist attractions and campgrounds along the Russian River where you can rent canoes. You will soon be crossing a bridge over the river, so if you have a camera handy, this is a good time to take a scenic shot.

At Wohler Road take a left. Here the road changes significantly. Traffic is infrequent and you are in the midst of orchards, vineyards, and a variety of shade trees. Wohler Road winds for a while and then joins Eastside Road at the Raford House, a bed and breakfast inn, which overlooks miles and miles of vineyards and mountains. The view is incredible. Wohler Road continues around and crosses another bridge over the Russian River. This is a good place to picnic down by the river or to take a dip. Canoes pass leisurely by, and we even saw some rubber rafts trying their luck. The river is quite shallow under the bridge and very calm, but quite barren with few trees.

Continue over the bridge and take a quick left at Westside Road. A sign tells you that Guerneville is 9 miles away. This is a beautiful road, carved through forests and vineyards. You feel as if you are far from civilization — until a car passes by. There are some easy climbs here with thrilling coasts down. Westside Road meets up with River Road to take you back to Guerneville. This side of the road, however, has uneven, rougher, and more narrow shoulders at some places, so watch out for them. The traffic speeds by pretty quickly. (Don't forget to stop by Korbel's on the way back.)

VARIATION #1: You might also consider combining the *Eastside, Westside Loop* to Healdsburg from Wohler Road by turning right on Eastside Road. This will add 21 miles to your trip. Return along Westside Road back to River Road, and continue as described above.

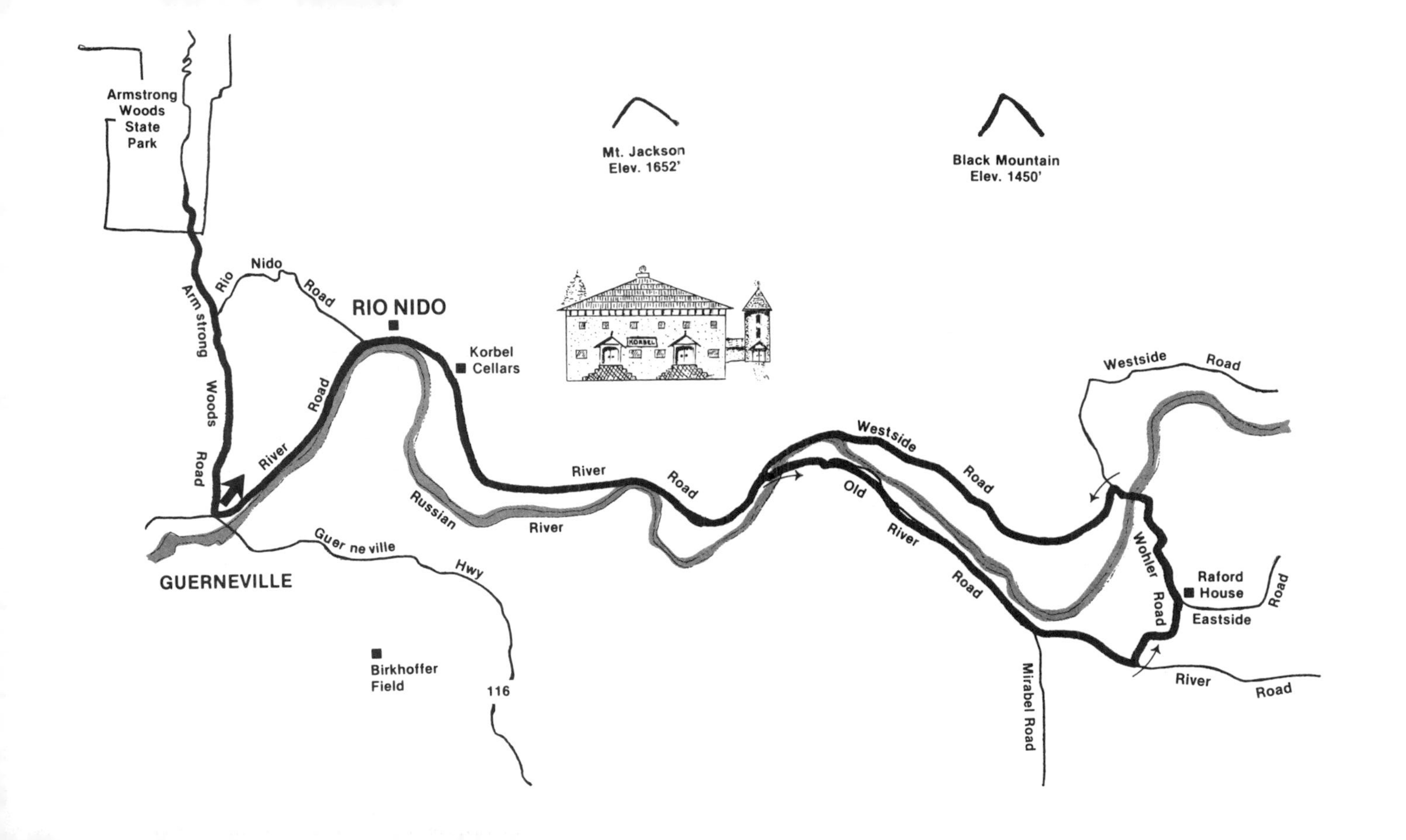

Armstrong Woods State Park
Mt. Jackson Elev. 1652'
Black Mountain Elev. 1450'
Rio Nido Road
RIO NIDO
Korbel Cellars
KORBEL
Arm strong Woods Road
River Road
GUERNEVILLE
Russian River
Guer ne ville Hwy
116
Birkhoffer Field
Westside Road
Old River Road
Mirabel Road
Wohler Road
Raford House
Eastside Road
River Road

12 HEALDSBURG EASTSIDE, WESTSIDE LOOP

REGION: *THE RUSSIAN RIVER REGION*

MILEAGE: *21 MILES (3-4 HOURS RIDING TIME)*

RATING: *MEDIUM DIFFICULTY — A scenic ride through forest and vineyards with beautiful panoramas of the distant mountain ranges. A basically flat road. Plan for ½-day to stop at wineries along the way and indulge in a dip in the Russian River.*

ROUTE: *From Healdsburg take Westside Road, 10 miles, which turns onto Wohler Road, 2 miles, and then left onto Eastside Road for 6 miles. Turn left on Redwood Highway which leads right into Healdsburg Avenue and the plaza.*

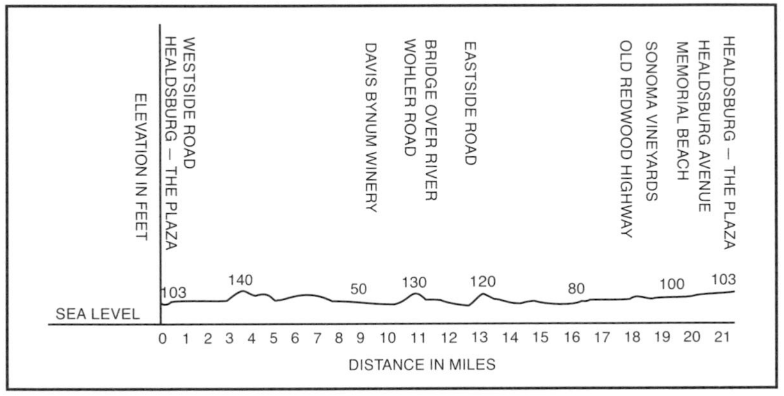

Begin your trip at the Healdsburg Plaza. Take Healdsburg Avenue to Mill Street and turn right. This is also the beginning of Westside Road. The road is busy and narrow and you will pass under the freeway and over what's left of Dry Creek — a gravel pit. The road now bears left and you leave the city behind and enter the quiet vineyard area. At your left you can see the mountain ranges many miles in the distance.

Westside Road is lined with oak, eucalyptus, and bay trees and the aromas accompany you almost the entire trip. The road widens now and becomes smoother where it was rather bumpy and narrow before. If you look across the vineyards you can just make out the telephone poles of Eastside. Road, your route back. You pass a gravel operation which sort of puts a; damper on the tranquility of the forest, after which the road twists and turns and is dotted with old farms and houses.

Hop Kiln Winery is on your left. They are open to the public on the weekends and, when this book was being written, was the setting for the movie, "The Magic of Lassie." Further on you will pass *Davis Bynum Winery*.

They have a small tasting area and delicious selection of wines that they will let you sample. The road becomes more densely wooded now and feels deliciously cool on a hot day.

Westside Road now turns right and takes you 9 miles into Guerneville. you may choose to take this road and return 17 miles later to complete the trip. If not, continue on Wohler Road, across the concrete bridge, and go for a short dip in the river. This may be a good spot to stop for lunch if you can find a shaded spot. It's rather barren along here.

Continue along this road and, at the crossroads at *The Raford House,* bear left onto Eastside Road. This road is similar to Westside Road, perhaps a bit flatter and more wooded. It will continue for quite a while. After you pass Kaiser Gravel Operations you will begin to notice colorful gravel trucks roaring by at express train speeds. They are large trucks and pass very close to the side of the road, so be careful! On your left lush valleys harboring miles of vineyards nestle below expansive panoramas of the surrounding hills. You can find Westside Road by looking for the telephone poles directly across the vineyards. After you pass West Windsor River Road you can kiss the gravel trucks good-bye. The road becomes smoother now and widens out.

At the stop sign turn left on Old Redwood Highway to Healdsburg. Shortly you will see *Rodney Strong Vineyards,* a modern and elegant building with picturesque pools and beautiful architecture. They have a large tasting room and you can sit at wooden tables while partaking of their large selection of wines. The staff will be pleased to answer any of your questions about wines.

Continue on Old Redwood Highway. You will be getting into heavier traffic as you approach the outskirts of Healdsburg. Pass under the freeway and you are on Healdsburg Avenue. Just before you get to the bridge you will see a sign saying *Healdsburg Memorial Beach.* This is a free beach where you can rent canoes. You might consider stopping here for a while to cool off and relax from your ride. You don't have far to go now. Once you've crossed the bridge you're practically there. The road will lead you directly to the plaza and your car.

VARIATION: You may want to extend your trip 17 miles by combining the *River Road Ride* and taking Westside Road straight to Guerneville, returning along River Road. This would comprise a 38-mile trip.

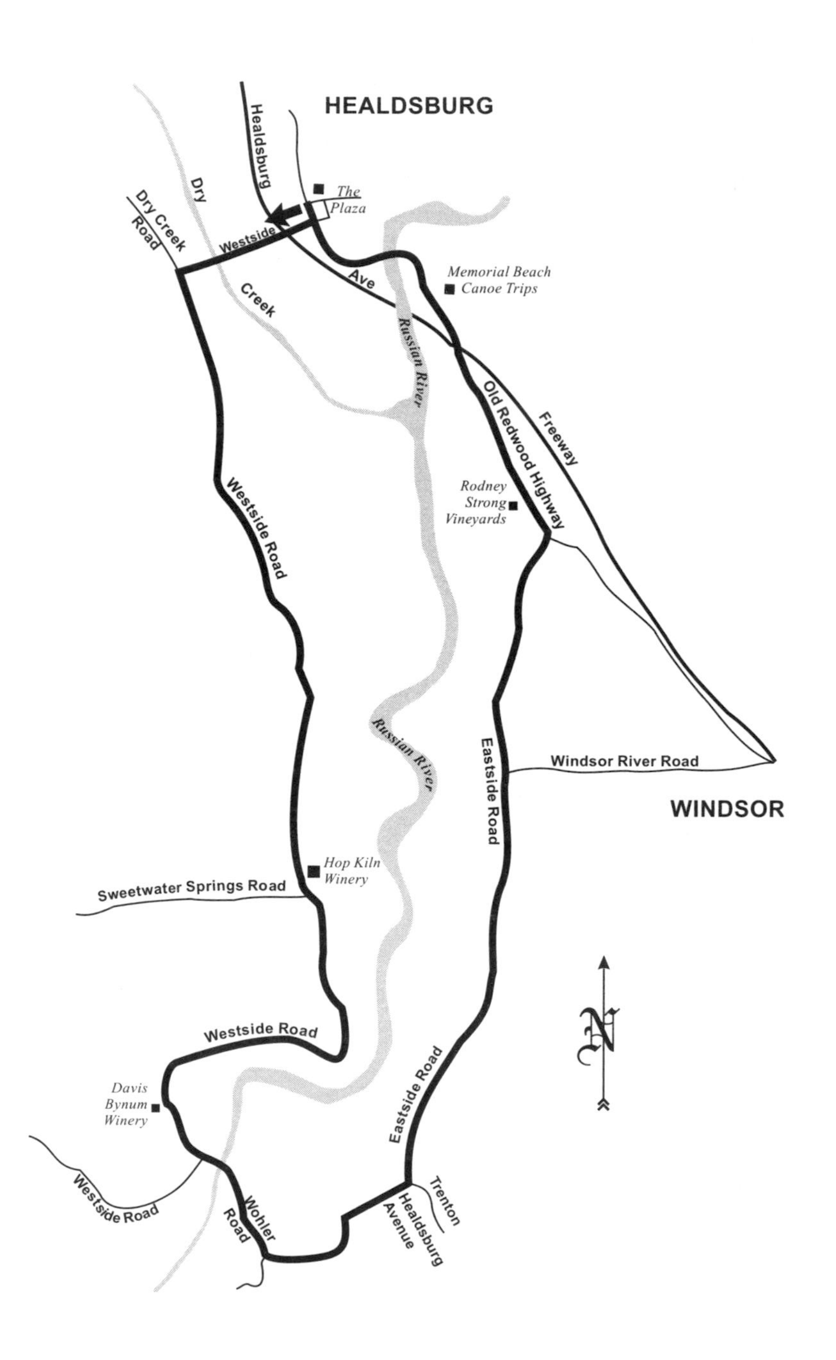
HEALDSBURG
Healdsburg
The Plaza
Dry
Dry Creek Road
Westside
Ave
Creek
Memorial Beach Canoe Trips
Russian River
Old Redwood Highway
Freeway
Rodney Strong Vineyards
Westside Road
Russian River
Eastside Road
Windsor River Road
WINDSOR
Hop Kiln Winery
Sweetwater Springs Road
N
Westside Road
Davis Bynum Winery
Eastside Road
Westside Road
Wohler Road
Healdsburg Avenue
Trenton

13 MONTE RIO TO CAZADERO

REGION: *THE RUSSIAN RIVER REGION*

MILEAGE: *20.5 MILES (2 - 3 HOURS RIDING TIME)*

RATING: *MEDIUM DIFFICULTY — Take a breathtaking trip through the tall, cool redwoods, along the picturesque waters of the Russian River and Austin Creek. Here the North Pacific Coast Railroad's narrow gauge line brought sightseers and vacationers from San Francisco to the "country" from the 1880's to the 1930's.*

ROUTE: *Take River Road west, 3 miles, to Austin Creek Road; Austin Creek Road north, 6 miles to Kramer Road; right on Kramer Road to Cazadero Highway; left on Cazadero Highway, ½-mile to Cazadero. Return on Cazadero Highway, 6 miles, to River Road; right on River Road, 1 mile, to Duncans Mills; left across Russian River and onto Moscow Road, back to Monte Rio, 3½-miles; left across Russian River on Main Street to your car.*

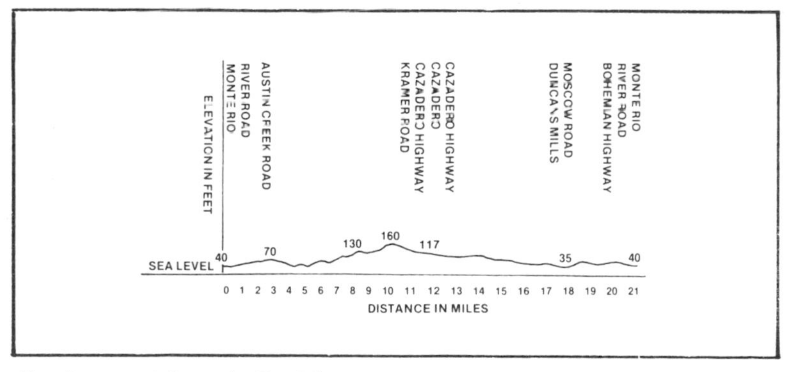

Begin your trip at the Rio Theater, on River Road in *Monte Rio*, carefully dividing your attention between the cars on one side and the redwoods on the other. After a brief winding narrow stretch the road widens and you'll soon make a right turn on Austin Creek Road where minimal traffic and the narrow road through dense groves of redwoods will make you feel like you are on a forest path. The gravel operation detracts from the view as you negotiate this part of the trip but helps keep the mouth of the creek open and supplies gravel and sand for roads, septic systems, and ready-mix concrete.

As the road crosses the creek and Cazadero Highway, be sure to stay on Austin Creek Road as it climbs above the Berkeley Music Camp. After passing St. Elmo Creek and a pair of one-lane bridges, turn right down Kramer Road and left on Cazadero Highway. The metropolis of *Cazadero* awaits you, sometimes called the "Heart of the Redwoods." The tiny town, once a logging community, has the *Cazadero General Store* and the *Cazadero Inn* as its central features. We stopped for lunch here where the food and service are good and the bathroom is a special treat. Cazadero is also the site of outdoor concerts which are staged in the *Cazadero Music Camp Redwood Grove.* It's easy to see why so many religious and civic groups have chosen this area for camp sites.

On your return trip you will find a nice mild coast back to River Road along Cazadero Highway. You can decide to return to Monte Rio by turning left onto River Road or continue on to *Duncans Mills,* our next point of interest. This was the site of one of the many now long-gone lumber mills of this area, and now is home for a small rebuilt town with interesting shops. If it's steelhead season, you may want to try a few casts in the river just a few yards from the town, where Freezeout Pool and Brown's Pool have been popular spots for years. You might also enjoy grabbing a picnic lunch and sitting down by the river.

To return to your car, cross the river and follow Moscow Road to the left. Stay on it until you reach Monte Rio. Back in Monte Rio there are a number of spots for snacks and several excellent restaurants for dinner in this area. If you finish your trip on a warm summer's day, a swim in the river from the public beach behind the theater will be just what you need before your journey home.

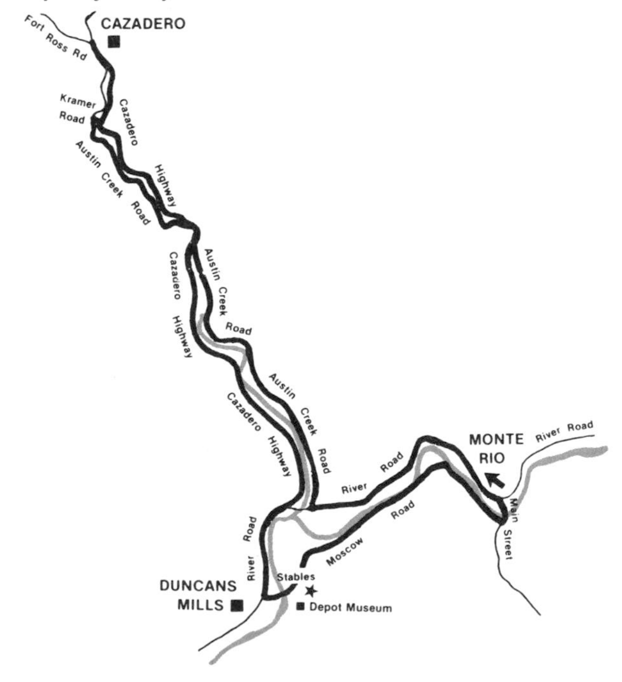

V. THE COASTAL REGION

ONCE BY THE PACIFIC

The shattered water made a misty din.
Great waves looked over others coming in,
And thought of doing something to the shore
That water never did to land before.
The clouds were low and hairy in the skies,
Like locks blown forward in the gleam of eyes.
You could not tell, and yet it looked as if
The shore was lucky in being backed by cliff,
The cliff in being backed by continent;
It looked as if a night of dark intent
Was coming, and not only a night, an age.
Someone had better be prepared for rage.
There would be more than ocean-water broken
Before God's last "Put Out the Light" was spoken.

ROBERT FROST

14 BODEGA TO BODEGA HEAD

REGION: *THE COASTAL REGION*

MILEAGE: *20 MILES (4 - 5 HOURS RIDING TIME)*

RATING: *CHALLENGING RIDE — Breathtaking coastal panoramas along winding mountain ridges make this ride a must. The initial 500-foot steep grade makes it difficult going for the average cyclist. Prepare yourself for fantastic views and a good night's sleep. An excellent trip for a picnic lunch at a scenic beach cove.*

ROUTE: *From the town of Bodega take Bodega Highway to Bay Highway. Turn right for 1 mile and right again on Bay Hill Road for 3½ miles, until you reach Shoreline Highway. Turn left for ½-mile and then right at East Shore Road. This will become Bay Flat Road. Turn right and follow it 6 miles until you turn left at Bodega Highway back to Bodega.*

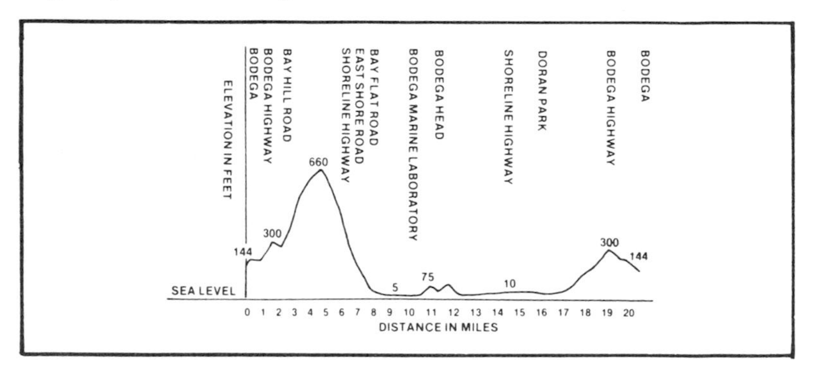

Begin your trip in *Bodega,* a quaint little town that was put on the map byAlfred Hitchcock's film, "The Birds." The old Potter School dates back to 1873 and is now *Bodega Gallery and Restaurant. St. Theresa's Church,* another landmark, was built in 1859. *Watson School Wayside Park* is a rest and picnic area around a one-room school house, built in 1856. There are several funky shops that make this town worth exploring.

Take Bodega Highway out of town to Bay Highway. The trip starts with a steep climb, even before you've built up any energy or developed a decent cadence. The climb is relentless and seems to continue forever. When you finally reach Bay Hill Road turn right and enter another world. You will find yourself surrounded by eucalyptus trees in a forest setting on a narrow country road. The smell of eucalyptus accompanies you on your ride. The road follows a dry creekbed on your left. Shortly the road opens up to a spectacular view of a mountain panorama with miles of barren hills. As you near the top ridge you can look to your left and view the first glimpses of the coastline and *Bodega Bay*, a small fishing village. Salmon, crab, and shrimp are major industries here. During the season, as many as 500 fishing boats are busily engaged in delivering fish to the processing plants on the harbor.

Around the bend you can get a direct view of the breathtaking Pacific, as far as the eye can see. A long descent puts the ocean right in your lap as you approach the stop sign crossing Shoreline Highway. There is a lot of traffic on the weekends and it goes by pretty fast, so be careful crossing.

Turn left onto the highway and follow it 1/2-mile around the bend and a right onto East Shore Road. This is a beautiful flat road that follows Bodega Harbor straight out to Bodega Head, the climax of our trip and a spectacular coastal vista.

The road is wide and smooth here with a bike lane only on the left side of the road; however, there are so few cars passing that going with the traffic is no real problem. On your left you will pass a day use parking lot for boaters.

A few miles later you will pass *Bodega Bay Marine Laboratory.* This is open to visitors Fridays from 1:30-4 p.m. The road seems to end by a chainlink fence, but a sign stating "Bodega Head" indicates how to get up to the vistas. Strangely enough, there are no other signs to tell you what you will find when you get there. It was only our curiosity and adventurous spirit that made us take that steep hike in 95 ° weather. You will probably have to walk your bike up the hill; but persevere, for just around the bend the road levels out and you are on your way to an incredible view. If you continue straight ahead the road will take you to a dirt parking lot overlooking the Bodega Bay entrance to the Pacific. Boats follow channel markers out of the bay because of its shallow depth. A sounding buoy rings every few seconds.

The road on the right leads to the coastal vista and offers a spectacular view of the waves crashing against the rocks. There are several vantage points to this view but be careful in windy weather not to venture too far along the cliffs. Tourists have been known to have been blown into the ocean. Hikers can follow the path down to a small sheltered beach cove, or they can climb the cliffs and explore the rocks. The views are magnificent and a picnic lunch is a must for this trip.

On your return, follow Bay Flat Road back to Shoreline Highway. Turn right onto the traffic and continue along this road back to Bodega. The shoulders are good and the highway smooth, but the cars go whizzing by.

This road follows the coast for a while and then turns inland. The hills around are quite barren near the coast but become more forested inland. Turn left at the sign pointing to Bodega and follow it back to your car.

VARIATION: If you are looking for a short, flat but spectacular place to bike for lunch, consider just taking Bay Flat Road to Bodega Head and back. Park your car near Sonoma Dunes and plan to spend an hour or so exploring the area. This trip is only 6 miles.

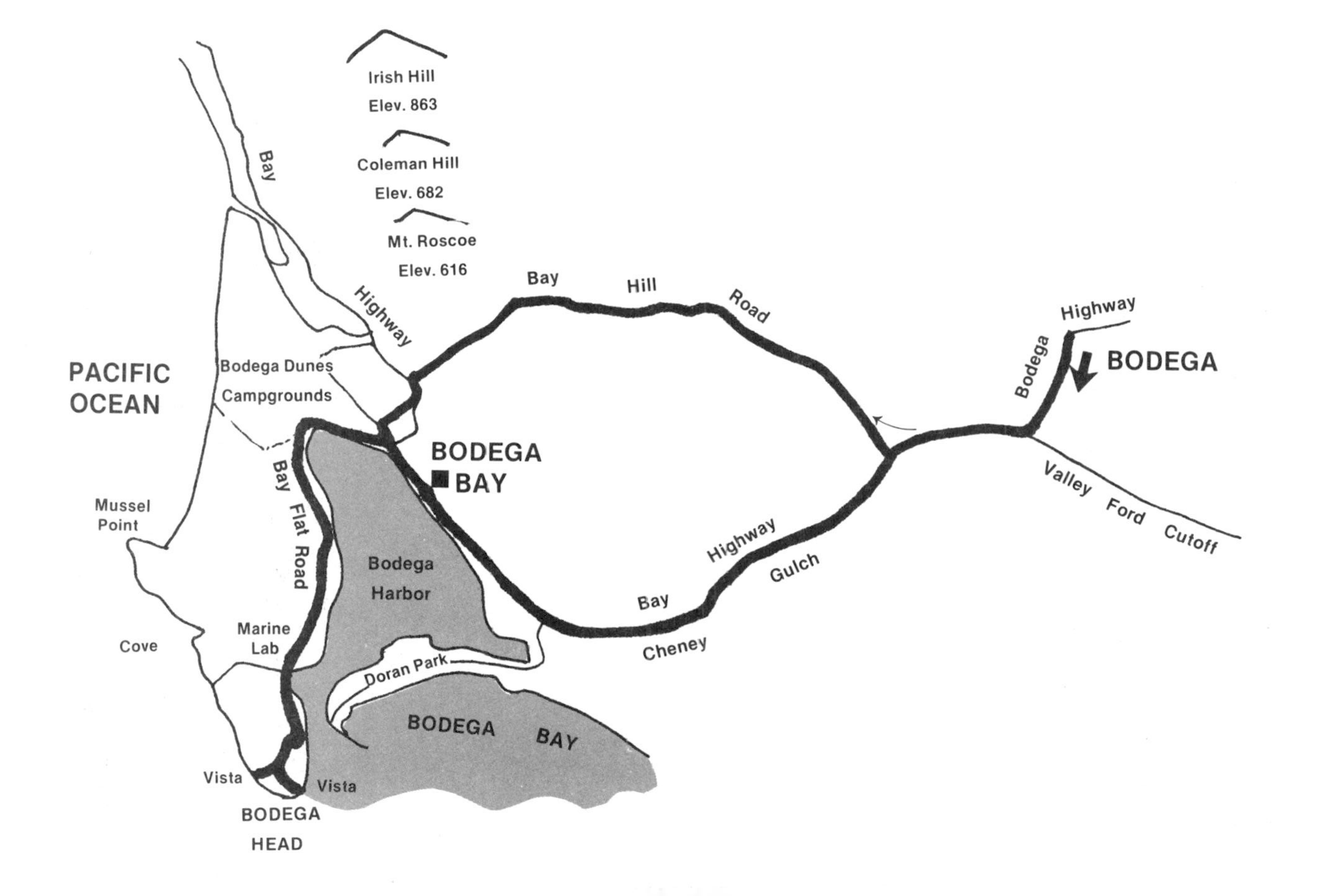
Irish Hill
Elev. 863
Coleman Hill
Elev. 682
Mt. Roscoe
Elev. 616
Bay
Highway
Bay Hill Road
Bodega Highway
BODEGA
PACIFIC
OCEAN
Bodega Dunes
Campgrounds
BODEGA
BAY
Valley Ford Cutoff
Bay Highway Gulch
Cheney
Bay Flat Road
Bodega
Harbor
Mussel
Point
Marine
Lab
Cove
Doran Park
BODEGA BAY
Vista
Vista
BODEGA
HEAD

15 *TOMALES TO VALLEY FORD*

REGION: ***THE COASTAL REGION***

MILEAGE: *17 MILES (3 - 4 HOURS RIDING TIME)*

RATING: *CHALLENGING RIDE — A spectacular ride near the coast with several fantastic views. Because of the difficult climbs in some areas, the ride may be prohibitive to beginners and children. Strong headwinds may also make this ride a strenuous one, but well worth the view if you're up to it. A morning ride when the winds are usually calmer would be more advisable.*

ROUTE: *Take Dillon Beach Road 2½ miles, which becomes Valley Ford-Franklin School Road at the coast, 6 miles. This road will lead you right to Valley Ford. Turn right on Valley Ford Road, past Valley Ford to Middle Road (Slaughterhouse Road) 1 mile and turn right again. At Whitaker Bluff turn left and then a quick right to an unmarked road and take that to Dillon Beach Road. Turn left to Shoreline Highway, and Tomales.*

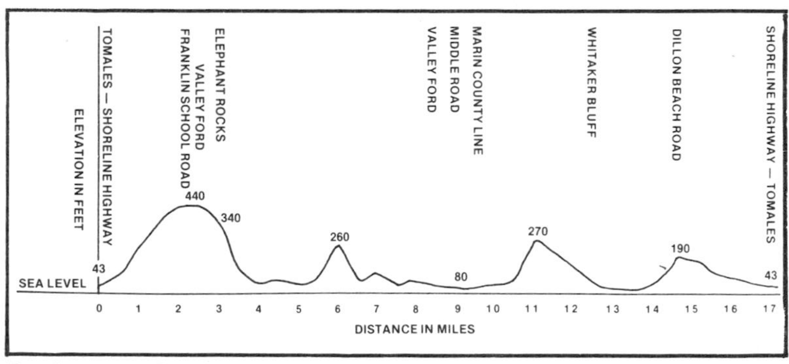

Begin your trip in the town of *Tomales*, a major dairy town, and take the Dillon Beach Road. This road winds through the residential outskirts of the town. Light traffic here allows you to study both the architectural design of these older Victorian-style homes and the variety of flora and fauna that surround them. Soon the road enters fertile farmlands amidst hills, bare but for brush and huge boulders sitting like sentries in the middle of nowhere.

The climb is long and tedious and will exhaust everyone but the most energetic cyclist, but the rewards are great. At the top you can see forever! An ocean panorama of extraordinary beauty discloses the entrance to *Tomales Bay* from a vast expansive sea. We happened to make the trip on a calm and exceptionally clear day. The water had not a ripple and the sky was clear blue.

At the Dillon Beach turnoff go just a few hundred feet to a vista described as *Elephant Rocks* because they do indeed look like huge gray elephants roaming the area. It is an excellent place to picnic after your long climb, or just to contemplate the beauty of the coast. A side trip to *Dillon Beach* may be desired. Be prepared for a steep descent of 400 feet and, you remember that old saying, "What goes down must now go up!" *Dillon Beach* has one or two privately owned beaches and an array of homes along small, narrow roads. If you wish to see Dillon Beach then continue down Dillon Beach Road. If not, then backtrack to Valley Ford-Franklin School Road and continue on.

This road has many spectacular views along it, but the going gets rough because the road is narrow and bumpy; however, there are few cars. A steep grade downhill can be dangerous along a winding bumpy road, so be careful! You can smell the eucalyptus groves and see cattle grazing on the relatively bare hills.

At *Valley Ford* be sure to stop at the *Valley Ford Market* and view the mural above the door. Christo's "Running Fence" put Valley Ford on the map in 1976 because the fence came right through the town, and tons of tourists flocked here for the two weeks it was up, to touch the cloth and follow it down to the coast.

Continue past Valley Ford and turn right on Middle Road, which is relatively flat compared to the road you just left. You will pass the Marin County Line and follow the road through shaded eucalyptus groves and small farms. There is a tough climb ahead, as you probably guessed. At the intersection take a quick left on Whitaker Bluff and then a right.

At the stop sign turn left onto Dillon Beach Road. This will bring you back the way you started, to the town of Tomales and your car.

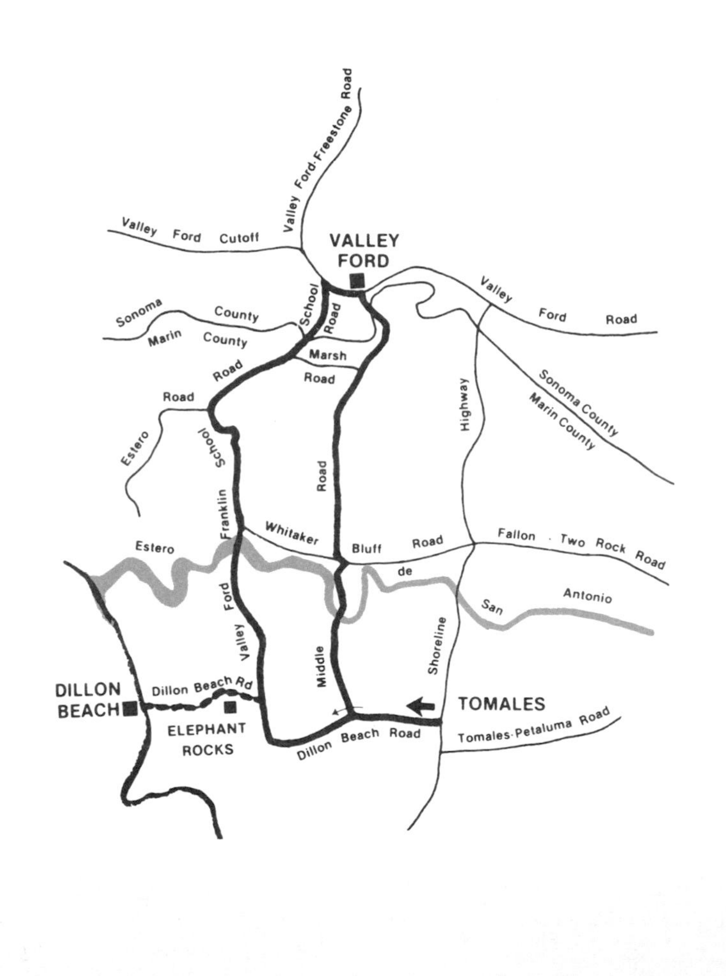

Valley Ford-Freestone Road
Valley Ford Cutoff
VALLEY FORD
Valley Ford Road
Sonoma County
Marin County
School Road
Marsh Road
Road
Estero Road
School
Franklin
Road
Highway
Sonoma County
Marin County
Whitaker Bluff Road
Fallon · Two Rock Road
Estero
de
San Antonio
Valley Ford
Middle
Shoreline
DILLON BEACH
Dillon Beach Rd
ELEPHANT ROCKS
TOMALES
Dillon Beach Road
Tomales-Petaluma Road

16 OCCIDENTAL TO THE COAST
"The Coleman Valley Experience"

REGION: *THE COASTAL REGION*

MILEAGE: *26 MILES (5 - 6 HOURS RIDING TIME — A FULL DAY! MAY BE CONSIDERED FOR OVERNIGHT)*

RATING: *VERY CHALLENGING! — A spectacularly exquisite ride that soars over the coastal ranges and spans hundreds of miles of scenic beauty that touch the very heavens! The roads are especially difficult with very steep grades that will exhaust the most aggressive cyclist. Only those prepared and conditioned for such a demanding ride will really appreciate its rewards!*

ROUTE: *Take Coleman Valley Road, 10 miles, and follow it to the coast. Turn left on Shoreline Highway, 1½ miles; turn left on Bay Hill Road, 6 miles, and left again on Shoreline Highway. Turn left on Bodega Highway through the town of Bodega and then another left at Joy Road. Follow Joy Road, 3 miles, to Bittner Road, and then turn right, back to Occidental.*

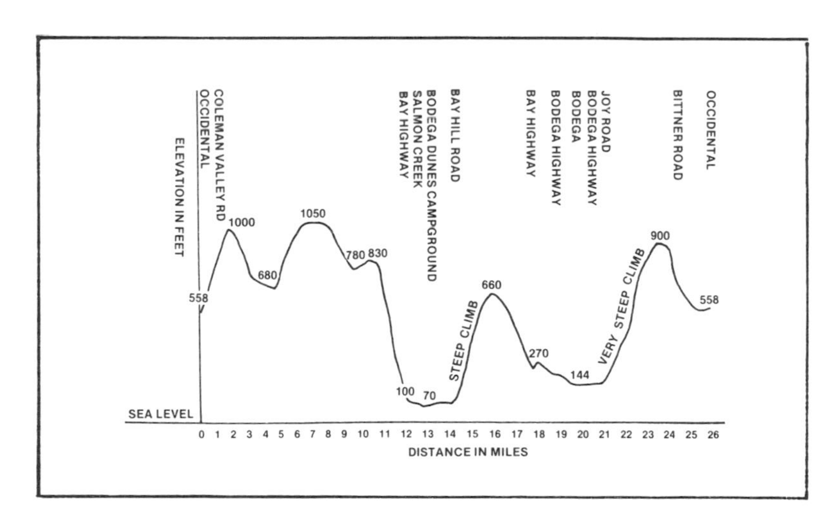

Begin your ride in the town of *Occidental,* a charming and colorful place. Coleman Valley Road begins right off Third Street in the center of town. The road begins to ascend almost immediately and gives you an indication of what to anticipate during the major part of this ride. It is a long, steep climb on a quiet wooded road that hopefully compensates for the exhaustion you will already be feeling. You will notice spectacular views on your right and the lush forest, as if you have ventured far from civilization. Hardly a car passes to mar the fantasy.

Suddenly the road opens out into a valley and then begins to climb again. Almost at the top (1,050-foot elevation) you will find a turnout (probably for overheated cars) that looks out over a vast expanse of fields and hills. The road is narrow with no shoulders, so be careful.

The road widens now and looks out over rolling meadows and vast sheep ranches. It was here that the Russians planted one of the first vineyards in the state in 1817. On a clear day you can see forever; on a foggy day you can see a few feet ahead of your nose. You will pass several cattle guards that prevent flocks of sheep from wandering too far. The weather can get quite chilly as you approach the coast; be sure to take jackets with you. Sheep can be found grazing alongside and in the middle of the road. Watch out for them.

As you get nearer the coast you can begin to see glimpses of the Pacific in the far distance. The road begins to descend rather rapidly now and gets quite winding, so brake carefully.

The descent ends at Shoreline Highway, a rather busy stretch of road (especially on weekends) that follows the coastline. Turn left here and reward yourself for your efforts with a breather on one of the turnouts. Either Coleman Beach or Salmon Creek have trails that lead down to the beaches. Here's a good place for a picnic and a dip in the ocean, if the weather permits. You might also consider camping overnight at *Bodega Dunes Campground* and returning tomorrow. If not, continue your trip by following busy Shoreline Highway for 2 miles. Turn left at Bay Hill Road. Prepare yourself for another series of steep grades with narrow winding roads and few cars. This road takes you along mountain ridges with deep, tight little valleys and quaint sheep farms. The road winds around eucalyptus groves and becomes forested and rough.

A stop sign suddenly appears at Shoreline Highway. Turn left here and proceed to the town of *Bodega.* The road is smooth here and has good shoulders as well as a few more cars, unfortunately. Turn left onto Bodega Highway which brings you right into *Bodega,* a little town nestled in farmlands with grazing cattle. It was put on the map by the movie, *The Birds.* The schoolhouse is now a bed and breakfast, but is still reminiscent of the eerie scenes in the film. Turn right on Bodega Lane to see it.

Continue through the town and turn left a mile up the road at Joy Road. The road is twisty and narrow and climbs steeply (200 feet in ½-mile to a crest of 480 feet. The road widens now and you find yourself in the midst of forest and redwoods. As you approach another major hill, and you think that you'll never get up another one again, spare yourself the agony and turn right on Bittner Road. It's a downhill coast to Occidental and becomes a two-lane road, so keep to the right. The stop sign at Scout Camp Road tells you that you have finally reached Occidental and your car.

VARIATION: If you want to take it a little easier on the return trip back, bypass Bay Hill Road and follow Shoreline Highway directly back to Bodega.

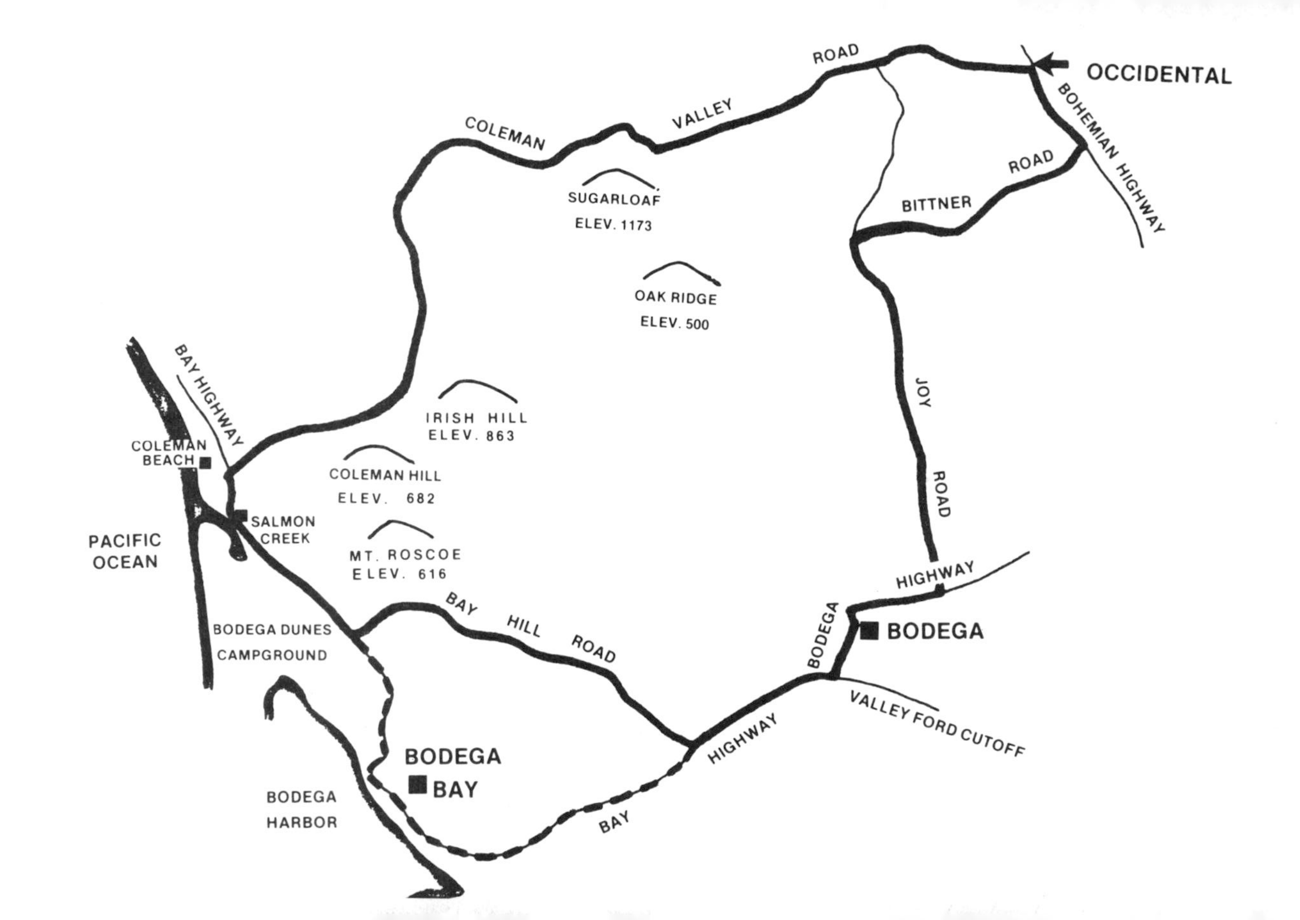

OCCIDENTAL
ROAD
COLEMAN
VALLEY
BOHEMIAN HIGHWAY
ROAD
BITTNER
SUGARLOAF
ELEV. 1173
OAK RIDGE
ELEV. 500
BAY HIGHWAY
JOY
IRISH HILL
ELEV. 863
COLEMAN BEACH
COLEMAN HILL
ELEV. 682
ROAD
SALMON CREEK
PACIFIC OCEAN
MT. ROSCOE
ELEV. 616
HIGHWAY
BAY
HILL
ROAD
BODEGA
BODEGA
BODEGA DUNES
CAMPGROUND
VALLEY FORD CUTOFF
HIGHWAY
BODEGA BAY
BODEGA HARBOR
BAY

VI. THE SANTA ROSA AREA

A MEMORY

Four ducks on a pond,
A grass-bank beyond,
A blue sky of spring,
White clouds on the wing;
What a little thing
To remember for years —
To remember with tears!

WILLIAM ALLINGHAM

DICKE

"Howarth Park"

17 HOWARTH PARK TO SPRING LAKE

REGION: ***THE SANTA ROSA AREA***

MILEAGE: *5 MILES (APPROXIMATELY 1 HOUR RIDING TIME)*

RATING: *EASY RIDE — Plan a fun-filled day with the entire family at Howarth or Spring Lake Parks by riding specially designated bike paths through forest woodland around Spring Lake. Then enjoy the many recreational facilities that the parks have to offer. Plan an evening barbecue or stay overnight at the campground at Spring Lake Park.*

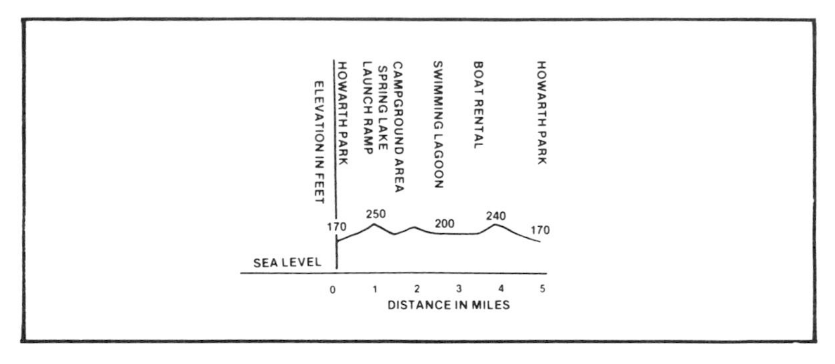

Begin your trip at either Howarth Park or Spring Lake Park parking area (Spring Lake will charge you $2.00 day use by car — free by bike). We started our trip at Howarth Park. A marked bicycle path specifies *Bicycles Only — No Motor Vehicles.* The path follows around the right side of Lake Ralphine and winds its way through wooded hills, leading you to the *Spring Lake Recreational Area* (approximately 1 mile). When you reach a fork in the road turn right to the campground or beyond that. Take a left at the stop sign to the boat launching ramp. The lake is used by small sailboats as well as kayaks and canoes, and sailboat races take place here often. Boats can be rented on the far side of the lake.

Continue through the wooden gates on the designated bike path around the far side of Spring Lake. Be sure to view the distant hills for a spectacular panorama of the area. The bike path brings you around the lake to the *Swimming Lagoon* area, complete with bath house, restrooms, concession stand and boat rentals.

The bike path continues from the parking lot adjacent to the boat rental and winds its way around the lake. A small climb brings you to the top of the main dam. Cross the dam for a nice downhill coast back to Howarth Park.

HOWARTH PARK: Offers lighted softball and tennis courts, picnic and barbecue facilities, hiking, biking and riding trails, and play apparatus. Big K Land offers miniature train rides, pony rides and a merry-go-round. Boating and fishing can be enjoyed on Lake Ralphine, as well as rowboat and sailboat rentals. Sailing classes are held in the summer. The animal farm, amusement park, and boat house are open during Easter vacation, on weekends, and daily during the summer months.

SPRING LAKE PARK: 320 acres, offers a campground, boat ramp, hiking, biking, and riding trails, picnic grounds, and a swimming lagoon. The shower rooms and concession stand are located adjacent to the swimming lagoon. The lake provides excellent facilities for small boating, fishing and picnicking. Barbecue pits and picnic tables are provided at various points around the lake.

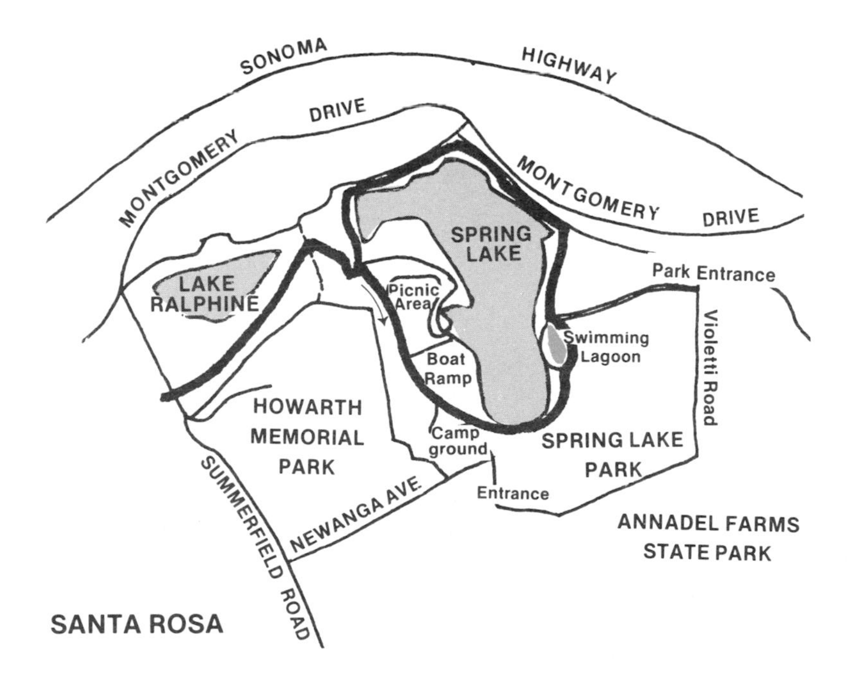

18 *BENNETT VALLEY LOOP TRIP*

REGION: ***THE SANTA ROSA AREA***

MILEAGE: *15 MILES (2-3 HOURS RIDING TIME)*

RATING: *MEDIUM DIFFICULTY — A scenic ride through the Sonoma Hills along pleasant country roads. The first part of the trip includes a relatively steep grade, but the rest is comfortably level. This trip might not be suited for children due to some heavy traffic on Bennett Valley Road.*

ROUTE: *Take Bennett Valley Road, 5 miles; turn right on Grange Road which then turns and becomes Crane Canyon Road, 3 miles; turn right at Petaluma Hill Road, 5 miles. Turn right on Aston Avenue and then left on Brookwood Avenue back to your car.*

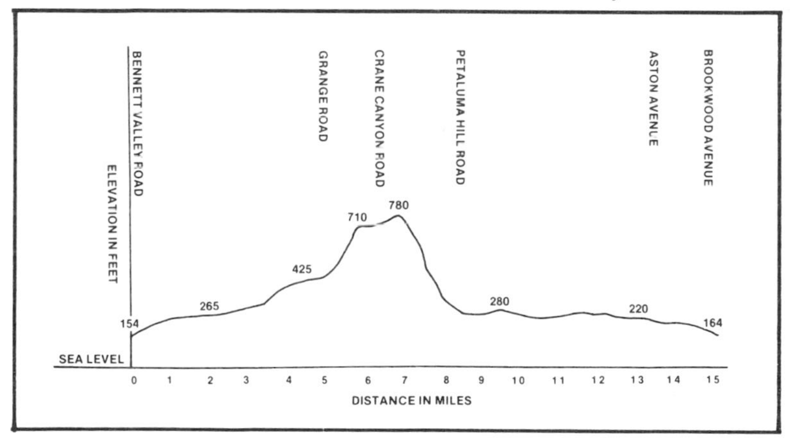

Begin your trip at the *Sonoma County Fairgrounds* on the corner of Bennett Valley Road and Brookwood Avenue. On Brookwood you will find ample parking for your car. Turn right on Bennett Valley Road to get out of the city. There is a bike path, but the traffic is relatively heavy for a while and, because of this, the ride is not recommended for children. As you reach the outskirts of town the road becomes forested and scenic. Traffic doesn't appear to be too heavy (we went on a Sunday) but the road winds around, making blind curves somewhat hazardous. On your left is the beautiful Santa Rosa mountain range — Sugar Loaf Ridge, Hood Mountain, and Bennett Mountain.

The road continues to wind and parallels the distant mountain ranges. You can see cattle grazing here. Turn right onto Grange Road. As soon as you turn, you are faced with an ascent through the hills. The panorama is magnificent with eucalyptus trees lining the road. Once the road becomes

Crane Canyon Road it indicates that you have finished your climb of 600 feet. Now it's downhill through winding tree-lined roads. Your coast ends at Petaluma Hill Road, a busier street with smooth, wide bike paths. A right turn here leads directly into Santa Rosa. As you pass the farms around this area you will notice advertising for *Crane Melons,* a delectable cross of Japanese melon that tastes like cantaloupe and honeydew combined. The melon was developed and grown exclusively in this area by Oliver Lawrence Crane in the 1930's, and the original family still lives in the area. The Crane melon is still produced locally and is ripe around the first of September.

In order to avoid the city traffic, turn right on Aston Avenue and ride on a narrow road past the rows of horse stalls of the fairgrounds. You might wish to explore the fairgrounds by bicycle. It is open to the public. You will notice the arenas, the many buildings and the racetrack. The fair is alive in July, while the rest of the year it is relatively empty with only occasional festivities and events on the weekends. The road will lead you back to Bennett Valley Road. Turn right to Brookwood Avenue and your car. If you want to bypass the fairgrounds, turn left on Brookwood Avenue and follow it directly to your car.

VARIATION: You might wish to extend your trip 10 miles and explore more of the Sonoma Hills by taking Bennett Valley Road past Grange Road and turning right on Sonoma Mountain Road. At the *Y* bear right onto Pressley Road which will take you down to Roberts Road. Turn right when you reach Petaluma Hill Road and continue the ride as described above back to Santa Rosa.

19 SANTA ROSA MARK WEST SPRINGS LOOP

REGION: *THE SANTA ROSA AREA*

MILEAGE: *15 MILES (2-3 HOURS RIDING TIME)*

RATING: *MEDIUM DIFFICULTY — A highly scenic tour of country roads winding through picturesque vineyards and shaded orchards. Many breathtaking panoramas of the St. Helena mountain range. There is very little traffic on most roads outside the Santa Rosa city limit.*

ROUTE: *Take Mendocino Avenue to Old Redwood Highway and continue until you reach Mark West Springs Road. Turn right until you reach Riebli Road and turn right again. Follow Riebli Road until you turn right on Wallace Road. This will lead you into Brush Creek Road and end at Sonoma Highway. Turn right and follow Fourth Street to College Avenue. Turn right on Mendocino Avenue to Bailey Field and your car.*

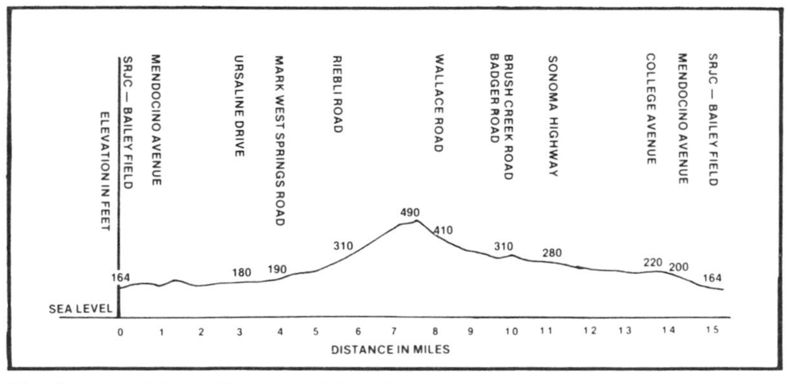

Begin your trip at Bailey Field parking lot at Santa Rosa Junior College on Mendocino Avenue. Cross Mendocino and proceed north out of town. Here you will be moving with heavy traffic and stop lights — and no designated bike lanes; however, the street is wide enough to accommodate both car and bike — if your luck holds out!

On your right, just beyond the busiest part of town, you will pass Fountaingrove Round Barn; on your left you will find yourself parallel to the freeway and K-Mart. Make a sharp right at the frontage road (it's not marked) and be careful not to find yourself in the middle of the freeway! Cloverleaf Ranch is on your right. When you see Orchard Inn make a right. This will put you on Ursaline Drive, a quiet, residential street. Make another right at Mark West Springs Road. Here you will find a good bike path and a long ascent to the country. Continue 1½ miles past a deer crossing sign and a billboard advertising *Petrified Forest — 9 miles*. (If you wish to make that trip, continue on Mark West Springs Road. If not, turn right at Riebli Road.)

Here our road becomes tranquil, lined with shaded oak trees and several attractive homes. Very little traffic passes by. Ahead you will find a vast panorama of the St. Helena mountain range. The road narrows here and becomes picturesquely dotted with small vineyards on the left. Watch for a curve in the road and a sign *The Foothills*, a large housing development; bear right and take a sharp climb. At the top is an open feeling of expanse. Rolling hills go on for miles. You'll make a sharp descent to a quaint farmhouse (it almost looks like the entrance to a small town, since the road runs right through the property), enjoy another panoramic view of the area, and proceed down to Wallace Road. Turn right and follow Badger onto Brush Creek Road for 3 miles. At the stop sign turn right on Sonoma Highway. And so we leave the country behind.

Sonoma Highway becomes Fourth Street, which is wide-laned and *busy!* Traffic roars by! Follow Fourth Street for 2 miles and bear right at College Avenue. Turn right again at Mendocino and continue to Bailey Field and your car.

VARIATION: You may be interested in taking the more ambitious trip to *The Petrified Forest* by continuing on Mark West Springs Road instead of turning on Riebli Road. This becomes Porter Creek Road and continues for 3 miles to Petrified Forest Road. Turn left for 2 miles until you reach *The Petrified Forest*. The Forest has been open to the public since 1860 and has a museum, picnic area and gift shop. It's an interesting way to spend an hour or two. For the return trip, backtrack to Porter Creek Road which becomes Calistoga Road and continue on for 7 miles, until you reach Badger Road. Turn right on Badger Road, and then left on Brush Creek Road. Continue the rest of the trip as described above.

To Petrified Forest
Riebli Road
Springs Road
Old West
Mark
Ursaline Dr
Freeway
Redwood Highway
Riebli Road
Wallace Road
Badger Road
Brush Creek Road
Sonoma Highway
Mendocino Avenue
SANTA ROSA
Cleveland Avenue
W. Steele Lane
Steele Lane
Santa Rosa J C
Guerneville Road
Fourth Street
West College Avenue
College Avenue
Fourth Street
Freeway
Santa Rosa Avenue

VII. THE SEBASTOPOL AREA

PASTORAL

If it were only still! —
With far away the shrill
Crying of a cock;
Or the shaken bell
From a cow's throat
Moving through the bushes;
Or the soft shock
Of wizened apples falling
From an old tree
In a forgotten orchard
Upon a hilly rock!

Oh, grey hill,
Where the grazing herd
Licks the purple blossom,
Crops the spiky weed!
Oh, stony pasture,
Where the tall mullein
Stands up so sturdy
On its little seed!

EDNA ST. VINCENT MILLAY

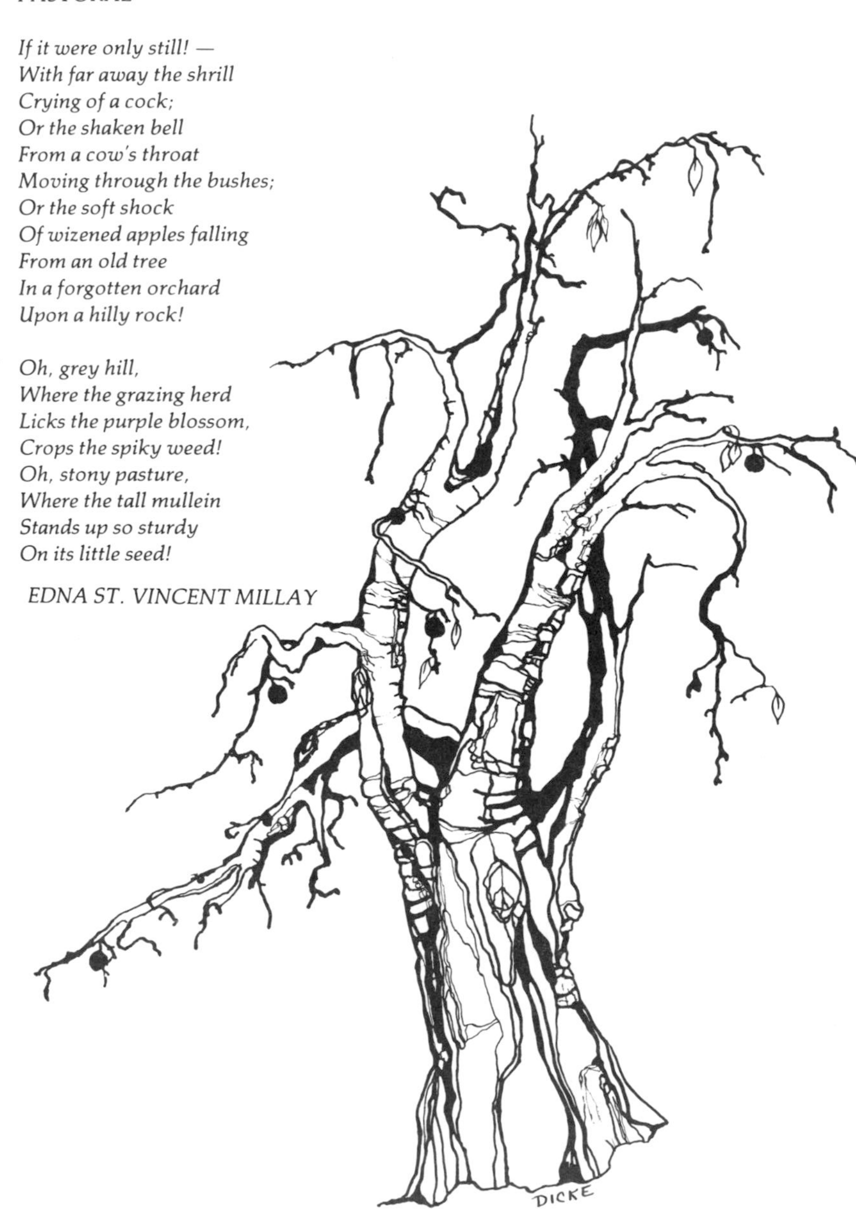

20 LONE PINE ROAD LOOP TRIP

REGION: *THE SEBASTOPOL AREA*

MILEAGE: *10 MILES (2-3 HOURS RIDING TIME}*

RATING: *MEDIUM DIFFICULTY — A relatively short trip in distance, but numerous rolling hills make the riding time considerably longer. The terrain is scenic, hilly and peaceful. A real chance to explore the back roads of Sebastopol.*

ROUTE: *Take Lone Pine Road to Bloomfield Road and turn left. Bloomfield Road becomes Canfield Road; bear left on Blank Road and follow it until it becomes Hessel Road. Turn left at Hessel and then right to Gravenstein Highway. Go across the highway and follow Hessel around and back to Lone Pine Road.*

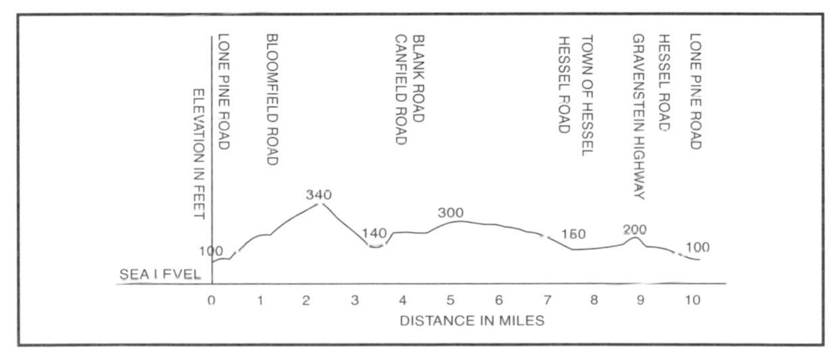

Begin your trip at the corner of Lone Pine Road and Gravenstein Highway. Lone Pine Road is a quiet country road with little traffic and winding hilly terrain. The road is ideal for biking because of its smooth surface and wide shoulders, but it can pose a problem for new or out-of-conditioned bikers because of its moderately high and frequent hills. It's worth the effort though, because of the splendor of the landscape.

Turn left on Bloomfield Road and follow apple orchards down winding narrow roads. Turn left on Bloomfield again and appreciate a panoramic view of the distant hills — brown in the summer and green in the winter. You will enjoy a free-wheeling coast downhill for quite a while. Turn left on Canfield Road and left again on Blank Road. Continue on Blank Road for several miles and bear left. At the stop sign take a sharp left onto Hessel Road. This will bring you to the tiny town of *Hessel* (if you ride too fast you will miss it). At the stop sign turn right on Hessel Road. This will take you to Gravenstein Highway. You can either turn left on Gravenstein to Lone Pine Road or go across Gravenstein on Hessel, which is just a small road, but one that will give you a beautiful panorama of the distant hills and then bring you back to Lone Pine Road and your car.

VARIATION: Expand your trip by turning right on Bloomfield Road to the town of *Bloomfield* and returning on Roblar Road. Turn left on Petersen Road until you reach Hessel Road. Turn right and continue up Hessel as in the previous trip.

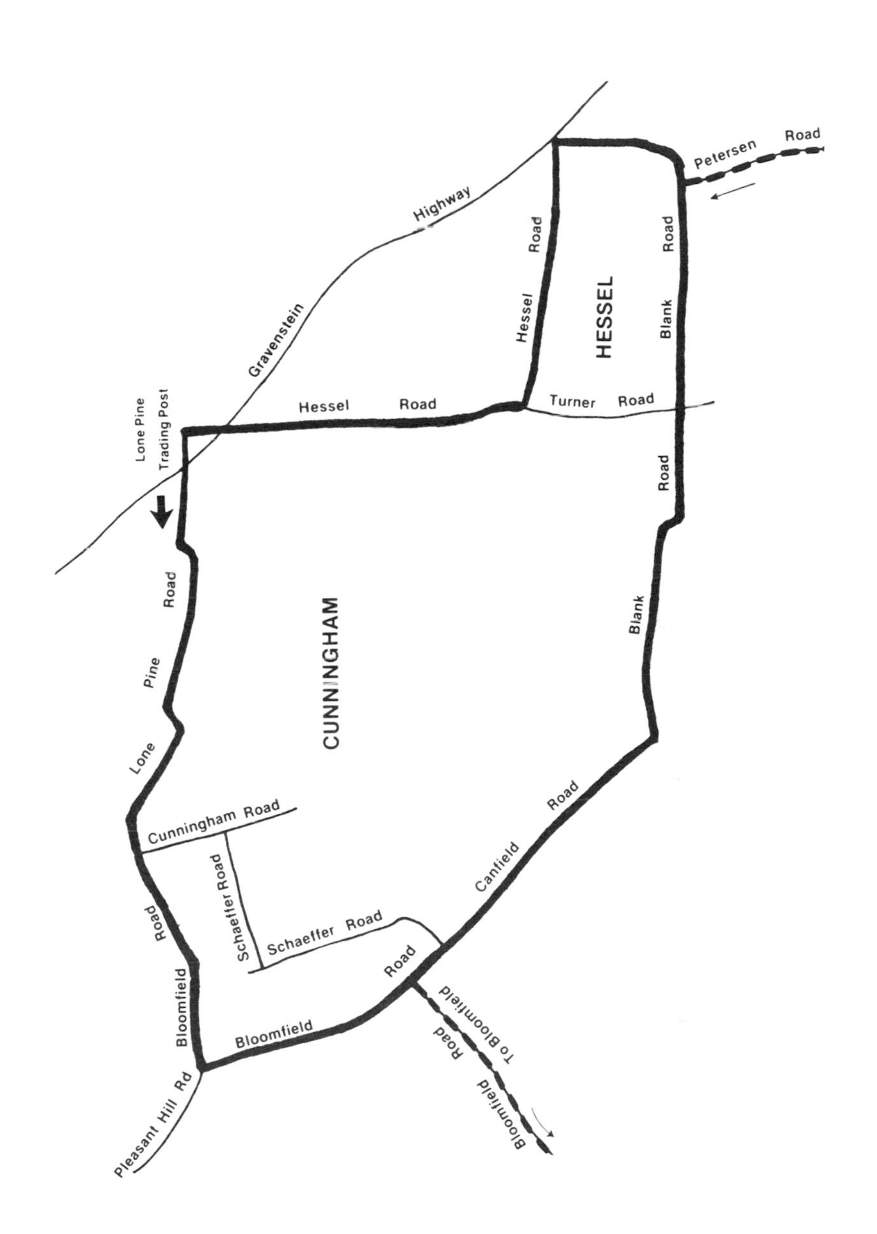
Highway
Gravenstein
Petersen
Road
Hessel
Road
Blank
Road
HESSEL
Hessel
Road
Turner
Road
Lone Pine
Trading Post
Road
CUNNINGHAM
Pine
Lone
Blank
Road
Road
Cunningham Road
Schaeffer Road
Schaeffer Road
Canfield
Road
Road
Bloomfield
Bloomfield
Road
To Bloomfield
Road
Bloomfield
Pleasant Hill Rd

21 FREESTONE — VALLEY FORD BLOOMFIELD TRIANGLE

REGION: *THE SEBASTOPOL AREA*

MILEAGE: *21.5 MILES (3 - 4 HOURS RIDING TIME)*

RATING: *CHALLENGING RIDE — A scenic ride through hills and valleys. Several moderate climbs and fairly long distance might become somewhat strenuous and therefore more suitable for experienced riders.*

ROUTE: *Take Bohemian Highway to Bodega Highway, left on Valley Ford-Freestone Road to the town of Valley Ford. Continue on Valley Ford Road, 6 miles, to Bloomfield Road. Turn left, 4 miles, and turn left at Blucher Valley Road. Turn left on Kennedy Road, right on Thorn Road, and left on Barnett Valley Road. Turn left on Bodega Highway and right on Bohemian Highway back to Freestone.*

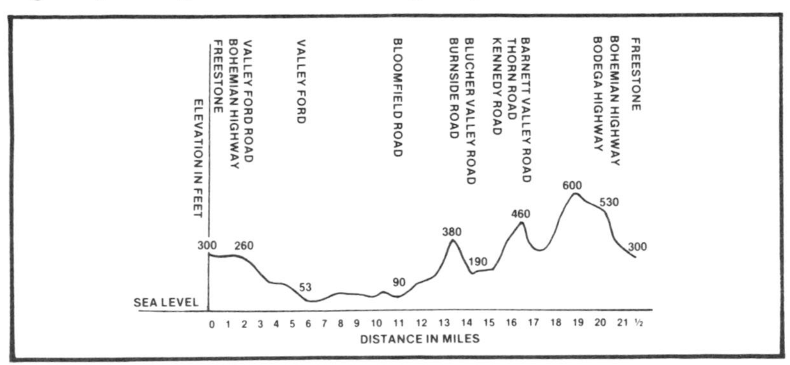

Begin your trip in *Freestone,* a village that got its name from the nearby quarry in 1880. The country store can supply you with picnic supplies for the rugged trip ahead. Wandering through the town is quite interesting. There are antique stores and museums, all nicely renovated and neat.

Take the main street, Bohemian Highway, back to Bodega Highway. It has good shoulders, and the road is wide and smooth. This will take you right to Valley Ford. As you approach the town the road gets a bit rougher and narrower with no shoulders, and landscape becomes quite barren with few trees. Then suddenly, the view expands into lush green (brown in summer).

Valley Ford is another tiny village with a modern bank and general store, and was also the central location for Christo's "Running Fence," which traveled right through the town in 1976 and attracted visitors from miles around who followed the fence to the Pacific. Over the store is a mural of the fence.

Continue on Valley Ford Road to get to Bloomfield. After the road passes Shoreline Highway it seems to smooth out and become more agricultural, passing large dairy farms. The aroma of eucalyptus trees gives the area a delicious flavor. At Bloomfield Road turn left. You immediately find yourself in downtown *Bloomfield*. Old buildings, mostly abandoned now, line the left side of the road while grazing cattle line the other. At *Emma Herbert Memorial Park* you can treat yourself to a picnic lunch and use the available restrooms.

As soon as you leave Bloomfield you begin your ascent through the hills. Eucalyptus trees line the road giving off a fragrant aroma, and provide shade for a hot and perhaps tired cyclist. At Burnside Road you can decide if you want to tackle a strenuous 500-foot climb in 2 miles for a fantastic two-sided view of the entire Sebastopol Valley, or continue on along Bloomfield Road until you reach Blucher Valley Road. Turn left onto a narrow road lined with funky cabin-style homes. The road twists and narrows but no cars pass along here. A rather tall, imposing hill looms ahead of you and you will notice large apple orchards. You can get a good view of the whole valley on your right (though I must admit not as spectacular as on Burnside Road). On a clear day the view extends for many miles and you can see the St. Helena mountain range.

When you reach Barnett Valley Road turn left. The road becomes forested and pretty as you approach a rather steep descent and wind down the mountains. Don't let the bike get away from you. Another scenic panorama of the whole valley unfolds at the top of another grade. It's really beautiful up there.

Most of the way back to Freestone is downhill. As you leave beautiful Barnett Valley Road and turn left on busy Bodega Highway you will truly appreciate the beauty of the area. A right turn on Bohemian Highway will lead you back to Freestone and your car.

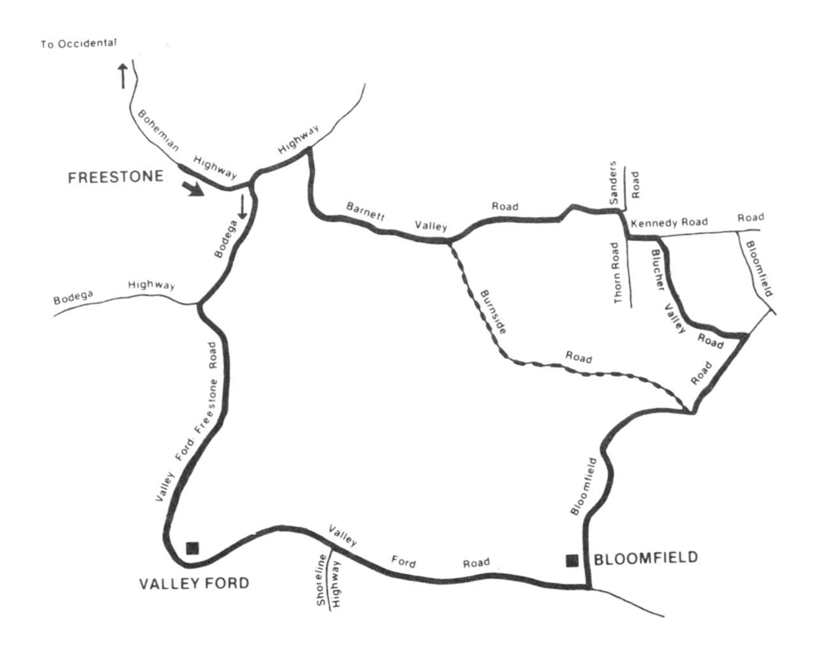

To Occidental
Bohemian Highway
Highway
FREESTONE
Bodega
Bodega Highway
Barnett Valley Road
Sanders Road
Kennedy Road
Road
Thorn Road
Blucher Valley Road
Bloomfield
Burnside Road
Road
Valley Ford-Freestone Road
Bloomfield
VALLEY FORD
Valley Ford Road
Shoreline Highway
BLOOMFIELD

22 *OCCIDENTAL TO FREESTONE*

REGION: *THE SEBASTOPOL AREA*

MILEAGE: *9 MILES (1 - 2 HOURS RIDING TIME)*

RATING: *MEDIUM DIFFICULTY — A relatively short trip through forested roads that can get rather steep at times. Some climbs are difficult, though the scenery is rewarding. A short but rugged ride.*

ROUTE: *From Bohemian Highway in Occidental turn right on Occidental Road at the north end of town, 2 miles. Turn right on Jonive Road and take that for 2 miles more until you reach Bodega Highway. Turn right and then right again on Bohemian Highway through Freestone. Continue on Bohemian Highway back to Occidental.*

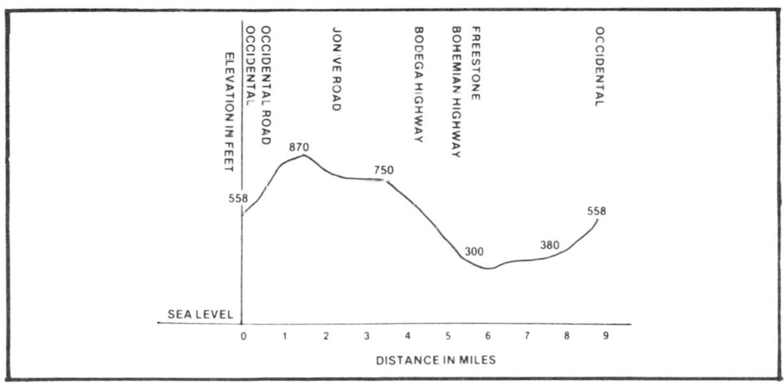

Begin your trip in *Occidental,* a great place to begin and end a trip because of its interesting shops and world-famous restaurants. Park your car anywhere in town and ride to the north end where you will find Occidental Road. It immediately begins to climb out of town, and the traffic tends to get heavy at times. This trip might best be planned for a weekday because Occidental is a favorite tourist attraction on the weekends. The road is smooth with an interesting feeling of wilderness, yet it is narrow with no place for bikes. The sign tells you that the next two miles are steep and winding. It is correct.

Turn right at Jonive Road and enter a quiet, forested narrow back road lined with homes and no traffic. The road peaks out after a while, and then it is downhill all the way to Freestone. That will give you quite a breather and a chance to take in the beautiful scenery. Some of the more impressive panoramas can be caught by peeking through fences of homes that have already staked their claim to the view.

Bodega Highway is up ahead. Turn right and then right again on Bohemian Highway, which passes through *Freestone*, a rather quaint small town lined with several antique shops and a country store.

Your trip back to Occidental is quite peaceful and shaded with only one mild climb on the entire road. It is forested with redwoods and there is a feeling of denseness, as though civilization has simply vanished. I really enjoy the smells and sounds of this area. Suddenly the road opens up and Occidental comes out of nowhere to greet you. Since the trip was so short, spend the rest of the day taking in the sights as a tourist and find out what makes Occidental so unique. Be sure to dine at one of the excellent Italian restaurants that boast of incredible amounts of delicious food — *The Union Hotel, Negri's.*

VARIATION: If you wish to plan a more extended 25-mile trip, take Graton Road out of Occidental and follow it to Mills Station Road. Turn right and then right on Ragle Road. Turn left onto Pleasant Hill Road until you reach Kennedy Road. Turn right on Kennedy Road, right on Thorn Road and left on Barnett Valley Road. When this reaches Bodega Highway cross it to Jonive Road and take that to Occidental Road. Turn left on Occidental Road back to Occidental.

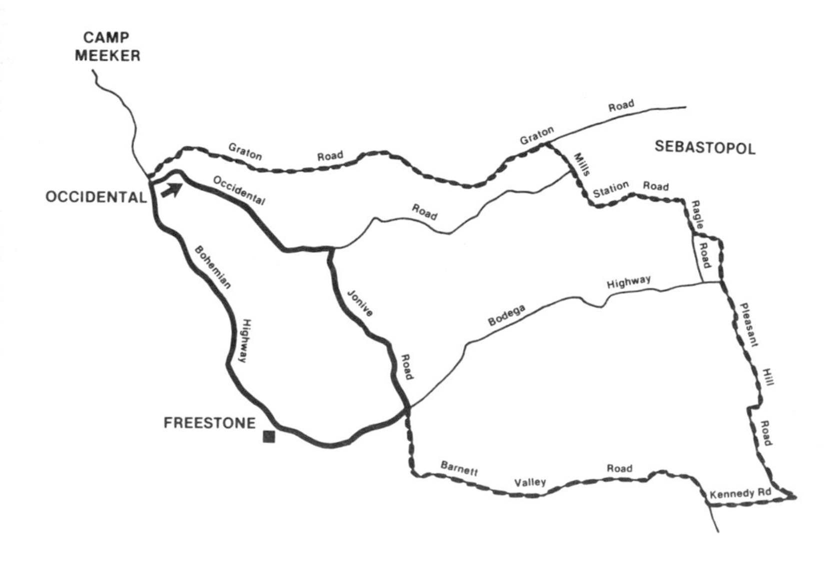

MOUNTAIN BIKE RIDES

State and regional parks are the best places to ride mountain bikes in Sonoma County. Be sure to check with a ranger regarding the current status of bicycle regulations in the area you plan to ride.

Annadel State Park* in Santa Rosa, has 5,000 acres of hills, streams, woodlands and meadows. Annadel is the favorite place for mountain bike riding in Sonoma County, with its 40 miles of dirt trails and panoramic landscape. Located on the eastern edge of Santa Rosa. *MEDIUM to CHALLENGING* *(See Ride 23 on page 88.)*

Austin Creek State Recreation Area — in Guerneville, has 20 miles of very steep trails, approximately 4-12 miles in length. There is no drinking water available. Located within Armstrong Redwoods State Park. *CHALLENGING*

Crane Creek Regional Park* — in Rohnert Park, has 128 acres of gently rolling pastureland and oak woodlands and spring wildflower displays, with an easy trail system for hikers and cyclists. Located East of Petaluma Hill Road on Pressley Road. *EASY* *(See Ride 24 on page 90.)*

Foothill Regional Park* — in Windsor, has 211 acres of gentle hills and easy trails through oak woodlands that circle around pretty ponds. Located at the intersection of Arata and Hembree Lanes. *MEDIUM* *(See Ride 25 on page 93.)*

Helen Putnam Regional Park* — in Petaluma, has 216 acres with spectacular views, as well as a picnic area with a small playground. Located off Chileno Valley Road. *MEDIUM* *(See Ride 26 on page 97.)*

Hood Mountain Regional Park — in Santa Rosa, has 1,450 acres overlooking the beautiful Valley of the Moon. The park offerss bicyclists an enjoyable wilderness experience; however, only the park's primary trail, which runs from the canyon floor to the summit at 2,730 feet, is open to bicycling. There is no drinking water available. The park is open weekends and holidays and closed during summer fire season. Located at the end of Los Alamos Road, 5 miles east of Highway 12. *CHALLENGING*

Jack London State Park — in Glen Ellen, has about 25 miles of trails available to mountain bikes. There is a 10.6-mile loop. One trail leads to a lake, approximately one mile from the parking lot. The trails go up the east side of Sonoma Mountain and are very steep. A large fire road leads to the back country. There are several vista points with picnic areas. The only drinking water is in the picnic area. There is a $3.00 day use fee for parking. *CHALLENGING*

Joe Rodota Trail* — in Sebastopol, using an abandoned railroad right-of-way, the trail crosses Laguna de Santa Rosa for 2.9 miles. The trailhead is located at Petaluma Avenue. *EASY* *(See Ride 27 on page 100.)*

Lake Sonoma Recreation Area — 11 miles northwest of Healdsburg, has a steep 4 to 5-mile loop on a wide fire road, which meanders along the ridge top, overlooking the Warm Springs arm of Lake Sonoma. There are two primitive camp areas, and a camping permit is required. During adverse weather conditions this trail is closed to bicycles. There is no drinking water available. Trail maps are available at the Visitors Center. There is no day use fee.

Shiloh Regional Park* — in Windsor, has 850 acres of woodlands, with 3 miles of hiking and biking trails. There are a number of steep grades and very rocky patches. There is no drinking water available. Located near the intersection of Faught and Shiloh Roads. *MEDIUM* *(See Ride 25 on page 93.)*

Sonoma Valley Regional Park — in Glen Ellen, has 162 acres of oak woodlands, and offers 1¼-miles of bicycling trails and picnic areas. The off-road loop has a slight hill and joins the paved walking path. The park is particularly beautiful in spring. Located 12 miles north of Glen Ellen, next to the Forestry Station on Highway 12. There is a $1.00 parking fee. *EASY*

Spring Lake Regional Park — in Santa Rosa, has 314 acres. This very popular park has an abundance of beauty and recreational activities, including a 72-acre lake, a 3-acre swimming lagoon, and miles of trails. The flat, paved bike path around the lake is 2.3 miles, and there are many more miles of dirt trails. Maximum speed limit is 15 mph. Located between Annadel State Park and Howarth Park. *EASY*

Sugar Loaf Ridge State Park — in Kenwood, has approximately 25 miles of trails that are open to bicycles. Most of the trails form loops, although some dead-end. As a whole, they are rather steep, with some grades as much as 20 percent. Many of the trails may be unsuitable in winter. The park gets very hot in the summer. *CHALLENGING*

West County Trail* — in Sebastopol, is the most recent addition to Sonoma County's bicycle trail system. Located at Morris Street and Gravenstein Hwy. *EASY* *(See Ride 27 on page 100.)*

For more information contact:

Sonoma County Regional Parks Department (707) 527-2041
California State Parks (916) 653-6995

*Ride is described in book.

23 SANTA ROSA ANNADEL STATE PARK

REGION: *THE SANTA ROSA AREA*

ROUTE: *MEDIUM DIFFICULTY (6½ miles) — A gentle ride to Lake Ilsanjo with a fantastic panorama of the lake and park. Begin at the parking lot on Channel Drive. Take Lake Trail to Lake Ilsanjo. Follow it around the lake, taking Live Oak Trail back to Louis Trail, returning on Lake Trail to the parking lot.*

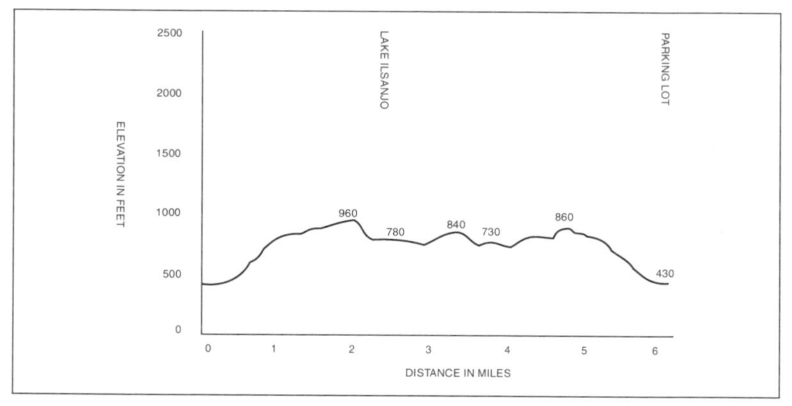

CHALLENGING RIDE (14 miles) — Ride to Ledson Marsh for a picturesque look at the park's wildlife. Begin at the parking lot on Channel Drive, take Lake Trail to South Burma Trail. Take a left on Marsh Trail and follow it around Ledson Marsh as it becomes Ridge Trail. Return on Marsh Trail and stay on it for a while. Bear right to Canyon Trail, left on Live Oak to Louis Trail, returning on Lake Trail to the parking lot.

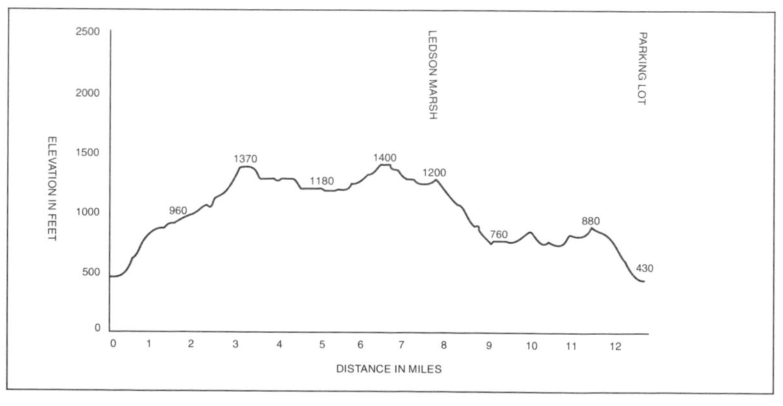

Annadel State Park, located on the eastern edge of Santa Rosa, has been a favorite area of off-road cyclists for years. Annadel offers 5,000 acres of excellent trails with rolling hills, intermittent streams, woodlands and meadows. There are 35 miles of gently rolling trails in the park with elevations ranging from 360 to 1,880 feet.

Lake Ilsanjo, a 2½-mile ride from the parking lot, is a popular destination for bicycles and hikers as well. The lake's Spanish-sounding name is actually derived from the combined first names of the property's former owners, Ilsa and Joe Coney. Restrooms are located along the shoreline near the lake and picnic areas.

Ledson Marsh, also a popular destination, is an ideal area for observing and photographing the park's wildlife, which include over 130 species of birds, as well as deer, fox, raccoon, muskrat, skunk, bobcat and wild pig.

Drinking water is available only at the park office; carry a canteen on your bike, as the spring water is unsafe. There are a few rattlesnakes, so be alert for them as well as for poison oak. Check the signposts to be sure you're taking the trail you intended to take. Camping in the park is not permitted. Fires, camp stoves, and barbecues are also restricted. Because of the high fire hazard, smoking is permitted only in designated areas. Garbage cans are located at various points along the trails.

Annadel asks that off-road cyclists observe the following rules: (1) maximum speed is 15 mph, (2) if visibility is less than 50 feet, slow to walking speed, (3) alert trail users ahead of you of your approach, (4) yield to horses.

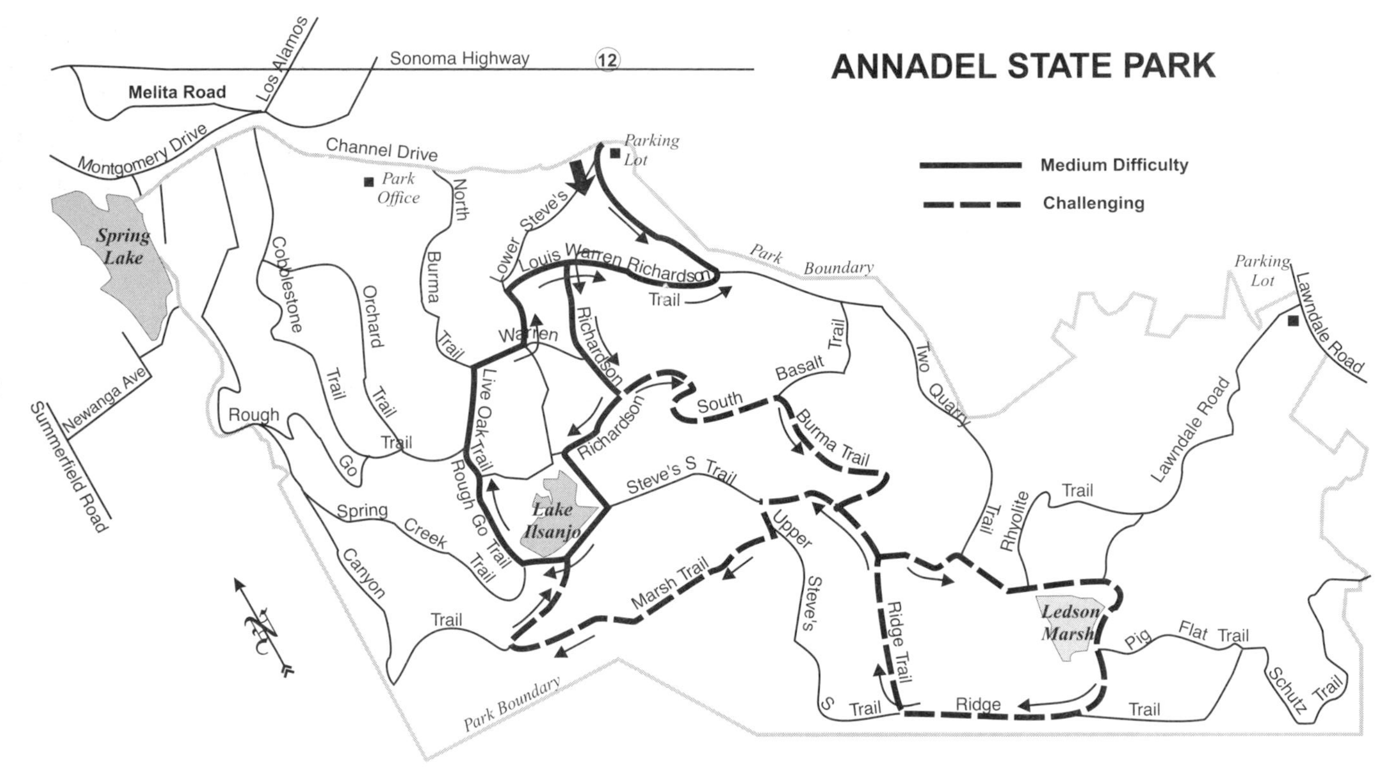
ANNADEL STATE PARK
Medium Difficulty
Challenging
Sonoma Highway
12
Melita Road
Los Alamos
Montgomery Drive
Channel Drive
Spring Lake
Newanga Ave
Summerfield Road
Park Office
Parking Lot
North Burma Trail
Lower Steve's
Louis Warren Richardson Trail
Richardson
Richardson
Warren
Live Oak Trail
Rough Go Trail
Cobblestone Trail
Orchard Trail
Rough Go Trail
Spring Creek Trail
Canyon Trail
Lake Ilsanjo
Steve's S Trail
South Burma Trail
Basalt Trail
Park Boundary
Two Quarry Trail
Marsh Trail
Upper Steve's S Trail
Ridge Trail
Ridge Trail
Rhyolite Trail
Lawndale Road
Parking Lot
Lawndale Road
Ledson Marsh
Pig Flat Trail
Schutz Trail
Park Boundary

24 ROHNERT PARK CRANE CREEK REGIONAL PARK

REGION: *SOUTHERN SONOMA COUNTY*

MILEAGE: *7 MILES (1-2 HOURS RIDING TIME)*

RATING: *EASY RIDE — The route to the park is mostly flat with a gentle hill just before you reach the park. Inside the park, depending on the trails you explore, there are some steep, short hills, but you can avoid them if you wish. A mountain bike is recommended for riding in the park. For those on road bikes, there is a bike rack next to the parking lot in the park where you can lock your bike while you hike and picnic in the park.*

ROUTE: *Start at Petaluma Hill Road next to Sonoma State University. Ride south, then turn left onto Roberts Road. Follow this road past Lichau Road (where it changes its name to Pressley Road) to the park entrance. Enter the park and explore the trails. The return is just the reverse of the ride in.*

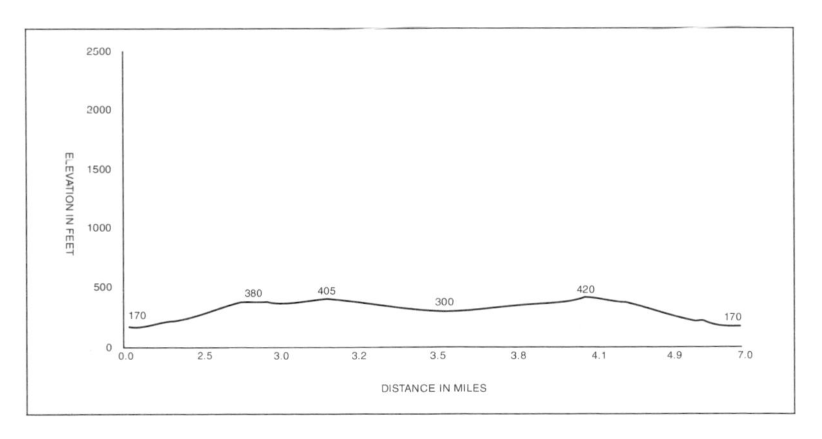

Park your car on the wide shoulder of Petaluma Hill Road. Before you start, be sure to bring plenty of water. Although this ride is short, it can often be hot in the summer and there is no water available in the park. Point your bike south and head down to Roberts Road, a little less than a mile. Turn left onto Roberts Road (watch out for the traffic) and leave the cars behind. Roberts Road winds its way for about 2 miles to the park, passing a number of mansions, somewhat incongruously set in the surrounding ranchland. At the intersection of Lichau Road, the road changes its name to Pressley Road, crosses a cattle grate, and winds up a small climb to the park entrance.

There is another cattle grate at the park entrance, but this one has a special path in the center for bikes to cross. The park is criss-crossed with trails. Road bike riders will want to lock up their bikes at the rack and hike in. Mountain bike riders, on the other hand, are well equipped to ride on the trails.

The main bike trail mapped out by the park service is located off to the west, marked by a gate out of the parking lot. This trail follows the periphery of the park, crossing Crane Creek three times. At the start, the trail climbs to the right, peaking at a very nice panorama of the valley below the park. There is a convenient bench there to stop, catch your breath and contemplate the view. Continuing on, the trail descends steeply, testing one's off-road riding skills. Less experienced riders will probably want to walk this section. Further on, the trail reaches a gate and, going through, crosses Crane Creek for the first time. The creek bed is rocky, and all riders are advised to walk across. From here the trail goes up a rise and bends around the shoulder of a hill. A very steep hiking trail branches off for another vista point. About 400 feet from the end of this wide trail (it just dead ends at an old gate next to Pressley Road) is a narrower trail (about 4 feet wide) heading back to the parking lot which crosses the creek beds. You'll need to walk your bike across because of the rocks. Total riding distance is a little over a mile.

Between the main bicycle trail, the park has numerous hiking trails. Most are well marked with rock shoulders and, for the most part, flat. These trails provide convenient access to picnic tables scattered throughout the park. After exploring the trails, return to your car the way you came for a total of seven miles.

VARIATION: For those looking for a longer and much more strenuous ride, cycle out to the park, as described above, but for the return, make a left turn onto Pressley Road, instead of right, when leaving the park. Very shortly you will climb up a steep grade that continues for 1.7 miles. The view is the reward! From here it is down to Sonoma Mountain Road, left and down to Bennett Valley Road. Turn left here and cycle past the beautiful Matanzas Creek Vineyards. A left turn onto Grange Road puts you almost immediately onto another steep climb. After about 1.2 miles of this fun, there is a nice place to stop, get refreshed and view Sonoma Mountain across the valley. Another ½-mile of gentle uphill and then it's a sweeping, steep descent to the other side. Watch your speed! This road, although generally well paved, often has rough spots and water occasionally crosses it from streams on the hillside. Once in the valley, it's a smooth ride back to Petaluma Hill Road. A left turn (watch the traffic again), another couple of miles and you are back at the start. Total mileage will be just under 14 miles.

Written by Rawls Frazier

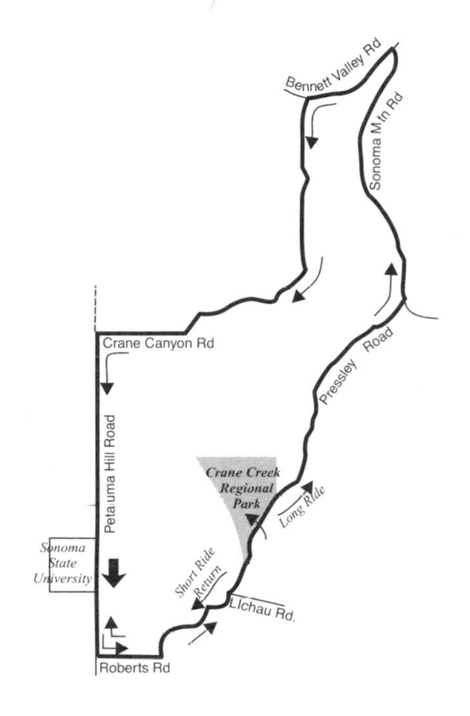
Bennett Valley Rd
Sonoma Mtn Rd
Crane Canyon Rd
Pressley Road
Petaluma Hill Road
Crane Creek Regional Park
Long Ride
Sonoma State University
Short Ride Return
Lichau Rd.
Roberts Rd

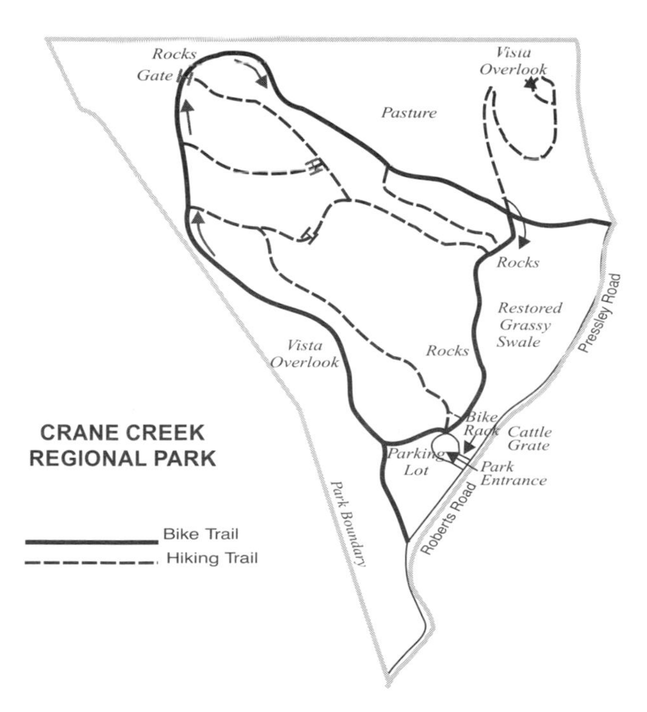
Rocks
Gate
Vista Overlook
Pasture
Rocks
Restored Grassy Swale
Pressley Road
Vista Overlook
Rocks
Bike Rack
Cattle Grate
Parking Lot
Park Entrance
Roberts Road
Park Boundary
CRANE CREEK REGIONAL PARK
Bike Trail
Hiking Trail

25 WINDSOR
FOOTHILL & SHILOH REGIONAL PARKS

REGION: ***NORTHERN SONOMA COUNTY***

MILEAGE: *12 MILES (1-2 HOURS RIDING TIME)*

RATING: *MEDIUM DIFFICULTY — Foothill Regional Park features gentle hills and easy trails that encircle pretty ponds. Shiloh Regional Park, on the other hand, has a number of steep grades and very rocky patches, making it a good place to develop and practice off-road riding skills.*

ROUTE: *Start at the entrance to Foothill Regional Park, where Arata and Hembree Lanes meet. Ride the 2-mile loop around the park, then cycle out of the park and head for Shiloh Regional Park, a little less than 4 miles away. Go west on Hembree Lane to Old Redwood Highway. Turn left, continue to Shiloh Road, turn left again and then right onto Faught Road. Shiloh Regional Park is 0.1 mile down Faught Road on the left. The loop around Shiloh is just under 3 miles. Return to the start at Foothill by retracing your route — Shiloh Regional Park to Old Redwood Highway to Hembree Lane.*

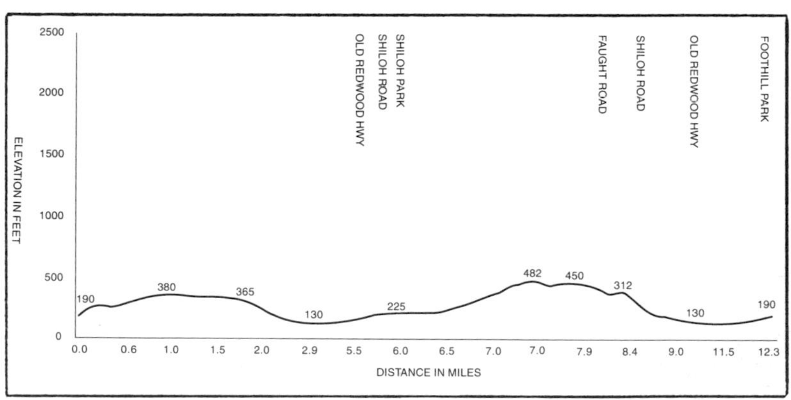

Because of their close proximity, you can do both these regional parks in one ride. Foothill Regional Park is a beautiful park of gentle hills, trees and placid ponds, nestled on the east edge of Windsor. There are many trails in the park connecting the three ponds which are its main attraction. The main trail out of the parking lot takes a short, steep pitch by the first pond and then weaves its way past the second pond. Just past this pond you turn left, head up a short climb and continue parallel to the pond. The route curves around and follows the periphery of the park, passing yet another pond outside the park boundaries. The trail continues back into the middle of the park, and then down and back to the start. You will find the trail has its ups and downs, but the surface is generally good and easy to ride on. Total distance is about 2 miles. Of course, you may be tempted to take side trips, so your final mileage may vary.

Back at the park entrance, head out onto paved roads to go to Shiloh Regional Park. Go left and head west down Hembree Lane. After 1.2 miles, at the light, turn left onto Old Redwood Highway and proceed to Shiloh Road, 1.6 miles further. Turn left and go 0.8 miles to Faught Road, turn right and, after another 0.1 mile, turn left into the entrance to Shiloh Regional Park. Shiloh has a much different look and feel from Foothill. Novice off-road riders should be prepared for steep hills and rocky, loose dirt trails. But, since the loop is not long, beginning riders should not be put off. It makes an excellent place to practice bike-handling skills and to build conditioning.

The trail out of the parking lot starts things right off with a short, but steep climb up to the main trail. Once there, a right turn puts you on a nicely wooded track for the next quarter-mile that is relatively flat. It then turns to the left, goes up a short, rocky climb and heads into a grove of oaks. The trail winds back around and down, and then climbs sharply up, culminating in a very nice view to the west over the valley. The trail continues to climb steeply in places until it reaches a ridge line that goes for about 1/3-mile. It then drops steeply down over loose dirt strewn with rocks of various sizes. At the end of this, the trail makes a sharp turn toward the west and drops further into more loose dirt and back to the parking area.

From here, retrace your route back to Foothill Regional Park, where you started. Without any side trips in the parks, the total mileage is a little over 12 miles.

Written by Rawls Frazier

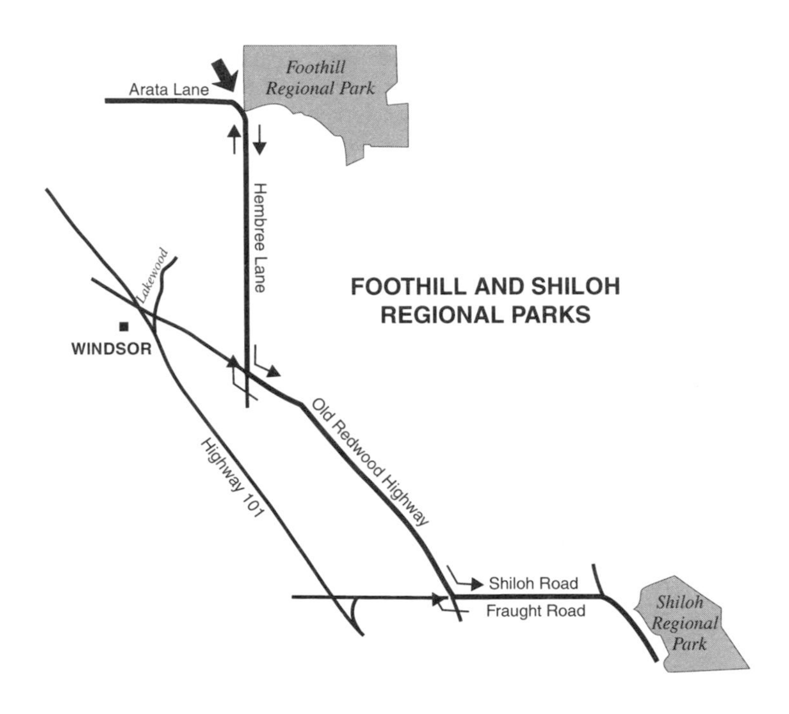
Foothill Regional Park
Arata Lane
Hembree Lane
Lakewood
WINDSOR
FOOTHILL AND SHILOH REGIONAL PARKS
Old Redwood Highway
Highway 101
Shiloh Road
Fraught Road
Shiloh Regional Park

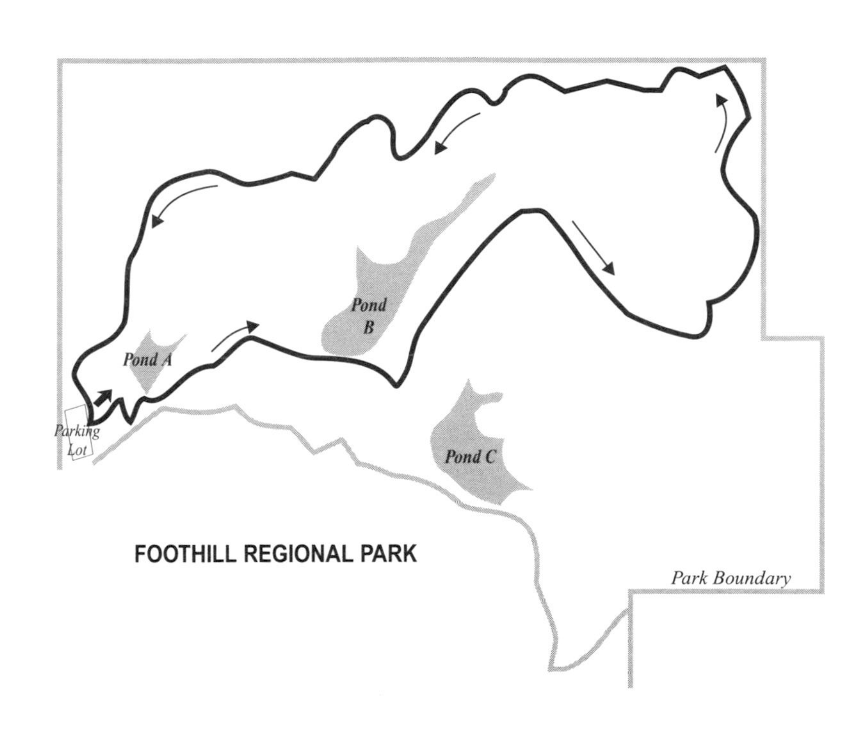
Pond A
Pond B
Pond C
Parking Lot
FOOTHILL REGIONAL PARK
Park Boundary

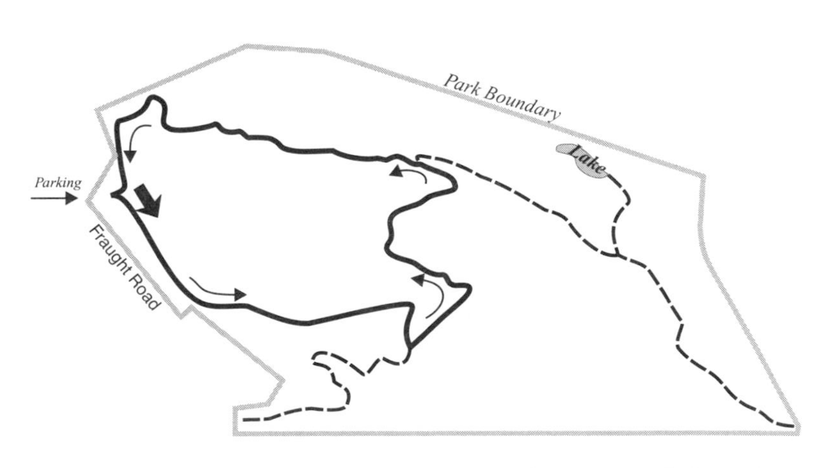
Park Boundary
Lake
Parking
Fraught Road
SHILOH RANCH REGIONAL PARK

26 PETALUMA
HELEN PUTNAM REGIONAL PARK

REGION: *SOUTHERN SONOMA COUNTY*

MILEAGE: *9 MILES (1-2 HOURS RIDING TIME)*

RATING: MEDIUM DIFFICULTY — A short tour to a nice park on the edge of town. The ride out is on paved streets, but the park is a great place for a novice mountain bike rider to practice off-road riding skills. Off-road riding in the park is a mixture of wide and single-track trails, some on easy terrain and some on steep hillsides.

ROUTE: Start from Walnut Park, ride west on "D" street and, at the edge of town, turn right onto Windsor Drive. Ride past the Victoria Homes and turn left at Western Avenue, left onto Chileno Valley Road, and left again into Helen Putnam Regional Park. Inside the park explore the various trails. A good first ride is to ride the paved road past the fishing pond to the crest of the hill where a broad, dirt trail crosses the road. There you can explore the two main trail loops — one to the south and one to the north. The return is out the other park entrance, left on Windsor Drive, right on Western Avenue, returning to Walnut park via Howard/6th Street and "D" Street.

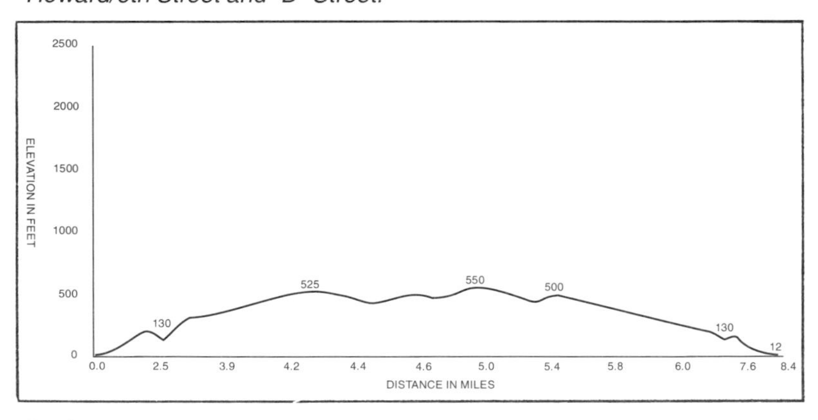

Begin your trip at Walnut Park, located at "D" Street and Petaluma Boulevard. On Saturdays in the summer you can't park next to the park because of the local farmer's market, so use a side street. From the park, go west on "D" Street, away from Petaluma Boulevard. The gentle climb up "D" Street takes you past blocks of magnificent homes, often used as backdrops for television and movies. One mile from the park turn right onto Windsor Drive. There will be a bit of a climb for about 1/2-mile and then a gentle downgrade until you reach Western Avenue. Turn left and, just under 1/2-mile later, turn left again onto Chileno Valley Road. From here it is just under a mile to the entrance to Helen Putnam Regional Park. Turn left and head past the parking lot up onto the paved path. This path is the main road in the park and goes for a mile or so. There are numerous trails to explore branching off this main road.

Ride up the paved path, past the fishing pond, until you reach the crest of the hill. A right turn puts you on the first trail to explore. A short but steep uphill through the oaks leads to the Helen and Ted King Memorial park bench, and a splendid view through the trees to the southeast. From here, the trail descends to another bench, with a sweeping view of grassy hills and cattle to the southwest. The trail then loops back and heads down into the oaks again. Here the trail becomes narrow, and you will need to watch out for low-hanging branches across the path. You will end up back at the paved road where you started.

Continue across the road onto the broad, smooth north trail. This route climbs gently upward and curves to the west. At the crest where the trail splits into four branches, take the turn to the north and descend into the oaks. From here you will basically follow the hillside contour and wind your way back around until you are parallel to the paved road and return to where you started. This and the first trail completes about 2 miles of trail riding. A number of other trails branch off the main trail that you can ride for more milcage. Some of these arc very narrow and go up and down steep grades, so you will want to exercise care if you choose to ride them.

Back at the paved road, head east down the hill toward the Victoria Homes. Turn left onto Oxford Court and left onto Windsor Drive. At Western Avenue turn right and head back into town. Turn right onto Howard Street (it turns into 6th street after a block or so) to "D" Street. Turn left at the light and return back to Walnut Park. The total distance, including the couple of miles on the trails, is about 9 miles.

Written by Rawls Frazier

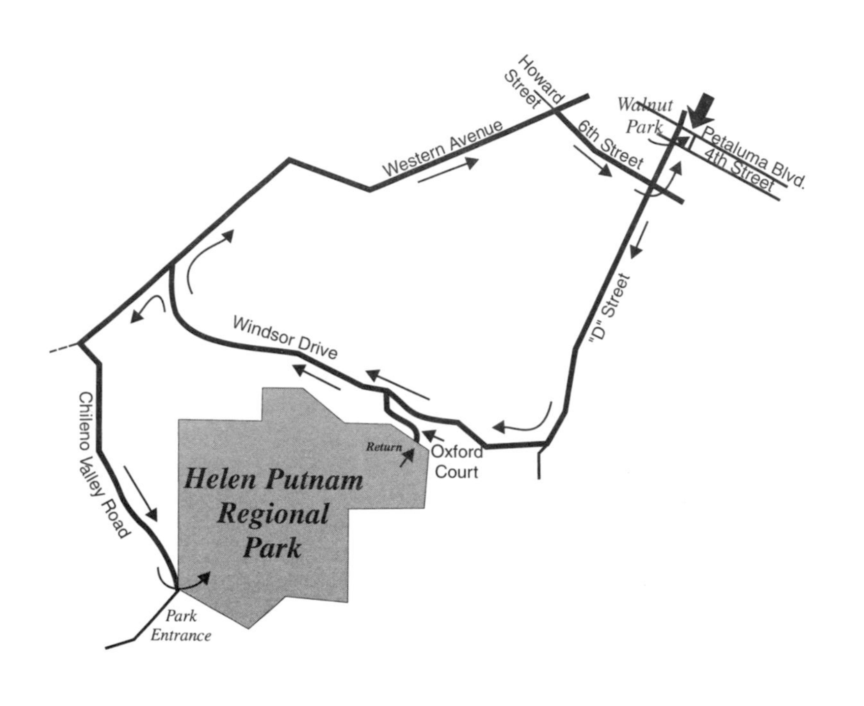
Howard Street
Western Avenue
6th Street
Walnut Park
Petaluma Blvd.
4th Street
"D" Street
Windsor Drive
Chileno Valley Road
Helen Putnam Regional Park
Return
Oxford Court
Park Entrance

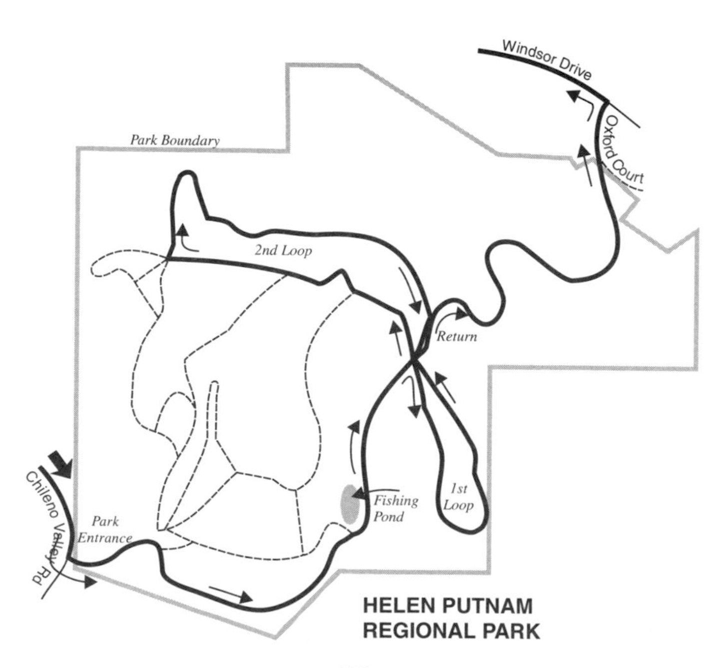
Windsor Drive
Oxford Court
Park Boundary
2nd Loop
Return
1st Loop
Fishing Pond
Park Entrance
Chileno Valley Rd
HELEN PUTNAM
REGIONAL PARK

27 SEBASTOPOL
WEST COUNTY & JOE RODOTA TRAILS

REGION: *THE SEBASTOPOL AREA*

MILEAGE: *11½ MILES (1-2 HOURS RIDING TIME)*

RATING: *EASY RIDE — Most of the route is relatively flat with a few gentle climbs. The Joe Rodota Trail, which is built on an abandoned railroad right-of-way, travels through a plain between Sebastopol and Santa Rosa, known as Laguna de Santa Rosa. The ride described here connects this trail with the West County Trail.*

ROUTE: *Start at the West County Trail entrance at Gravenstein Highway, and go to the trail end, where North Main Street and High School Road meet at Analy High School. Turn left onto High School Road, followed by a right onto Occidental Road, and then another right onto Fulton Road. After crossing Highway 12, a right turn onto Chico Road leads to the entrance to the Joe Rodota Trail, at the intersection with Merced Avenue. The Joe Rodota Trail takes you back to Petaluma Avenue in Sebastopol. A right turn here leads to a short, left-bending connection back to North Main Street. At the next light, bear right to reconnect with the West County Trail and the return back to the start.*

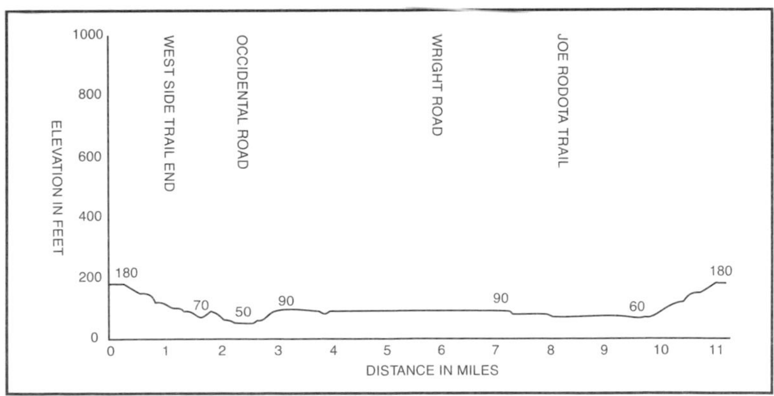

Begin your trip at the entrance to the West County Trail on the Gravenstein Highway (Route 116), just to the northwest of downtown Sebastopol. This trail winds peacefully through the trees for about one mile and ends at the entrance to Analy High School, across the street. Here, make a left turn onto High School Road (to the right the street is called North Main) and ride to Occidental Road, a little under two miles away. Turn right onto Occidental Road and cycle to Fulton Road. Turn right again and cross Highway 12 at the light.

On the other side, the road is named South Wright Road, and the second right from the light is a short, country lane called Chico Road. The right turn here takes you to the entrance of the Joe Rodota Trail. This paved trail is wide, smooth and flat. Built on an old railroad right-of-way, it provides a pleasant, bucolic ride just under three miles through the broad Laguna de Santa Rosa plain back to Sebastopol.

In Sebastopol the trail ends somewhat abruptly on Petaluma Avenue, which is part of Highway 116. This is a busy road, so one needs to be vigilant while riding on it. Take a right turn (the road is one-way here), proceed through the light and follow the road as it bends to the left and reconnects to North Main Street at the next light, about 0.3 miles from the trail. Turn right and, after about 0.2 miles, bear right at the light to stay on North Main Street, leaving the hustle and bustle of the town.

Continue to the West County Trail entrance, across from Analy High School, where you were earlier in the ride. Return back to your starting point along the trail.

Written by Rawls Frazier

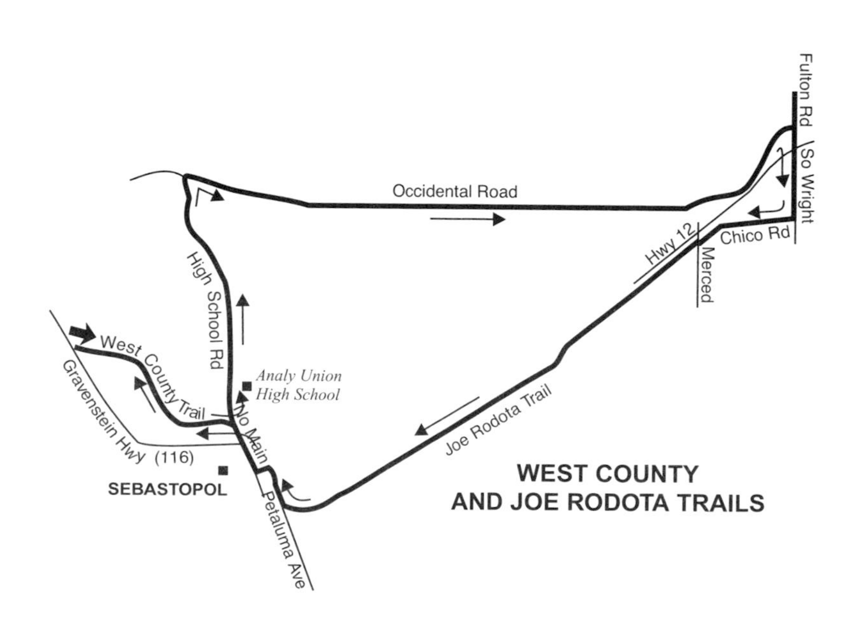

28 OCCIDENTAL WILLOW CREEK RIDE

REGION: *THE RUSSIAN RIVER REGION*

MILEAGE: *27 MILES (4-5 HOURS RIDING TIME)*

RATING: *CHALLENGING — Although much of this ride is on paved roads, you'll put your mountain bike to good use! The off-road portion starts high, with a splendid view out toward the ocean, then winds downward on a quiet, forested road before connecting again with the road at the Russian River. There is some serious climbing at the start and end of this ride, but that is more than made up by the rest of the ride, which is moderate and affords plenty of opportunity to stop and explore the sights and other attractions.*

ROUTE: *Take Coleman Valley Road west out of Occidental, right at Willow Creek Road, right onto the Coast Highway (State Route 1), right onto Highway 116, cross the Russian River at Duncans Mills to Moscow Road, right onto the Bohemian Highway at Monte Rio, and back to Occidental.*

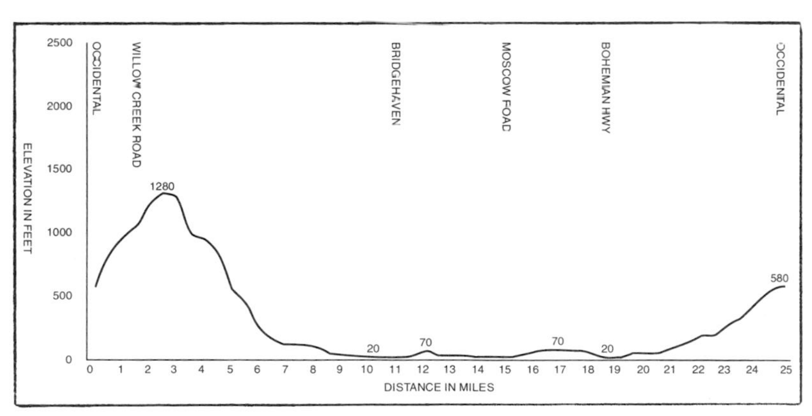

Begin your trip in Occidental, a small hamlet tucked within a set of forested hills. Coleman Valley Road heads west, out from the middle of town. It is uphill right away, so start in a low gear! The grade is steep for the first mile or so. It tapers off significantly as you come out of the woods into a broad meadow, and then starts to climb again as you get back into the trees. Just after re-entering the trees, make a right turn onto Willow Creek Road. You descend a bit but, as the road narrows, you'll head back up once again — fortunately at a somewhat gentler grade than the start.

The road here is in a heavy forest with little traffic. About three miles into the ride you will pass the crest of the hill and be free of climbing for awhile. After another mile, a sharp set of downhill turns in the trees takes you out of the forest and to the end of the pavement. At this point, it's worth a stop to admire the view of the valley spread out in front of you. Off in the distance to the northwest, at the mouth of the valley, you can catch a glimpse of the ocean.

The first mile of dirt road is pretty smooth, although in a few places around turns gravel has been added to stabilize the road. As the descent enters a section heavily forested with oaks and bays, it becomes steep again with switchbacks, looser dirt and rough road sections. You'll need to be extra cautious here. The descent continues for a couple of miles and then levels out to a delightful, creek-level trail, although you won't see the creek as it is buried in the trees. After about five miles total of riding, you'll reach a farmhouse (watch out for cows on the road!) and pavement again.

Here the ride opens into marsh land with thick stands of willows. At one end of this area is the Pomo Canyon Campground and, at the other, on the Russian River, is Willow Creek Campground. There are a number of places to pull over near the river for a refreshing stop.

At the 12-mile mark, Willow Creek Road junctions with famous Highway 1, at the tiny village of Bridgehaven. A right turn takes you across the Russian River. Bear right onto Highway 116, heading toward Guerneville. Except for a small hill just after this turn, the road winds its way just above river level until you reach Duncans Mill, a tourist stop in a wide clearing on the road.

Crossing the river once again puts you on Moscow Road and, after about ½-mile, back into the forests again. Here you cycle on a flat course through *Villa Grande* and on to the summer resort town of *Monte Rio,* with its fine beaches for swimming and sunning on the river. A right turn puts you onto Bohemian Highway, headed back to Occidental.

Most of this road is a gentle upgrade along the Dutch Bill Creek. At the beginning you'll pass *Bohemian Grove,* location of the famous (or infamous, depending on your political point of view) all-men's *Bohemian Club*, where wealthy businessmen and politicians come for retreats. There are also many summer camps located here, the most prominent being Camp Meeker, with its large sign strung across the road. Just before Camp Meeker, the grade gets steep again for the last push into Occidental.

Although the road is narrow here, it is nicely shaded and, just as the trees give way, the climbing does too, and you're back where you started. To finish off your day, there are a number of places to dine in Occidental, including the historic *Union Hotel*, which serves traditional family-style Italian meals.

Written by Rawls Frazier

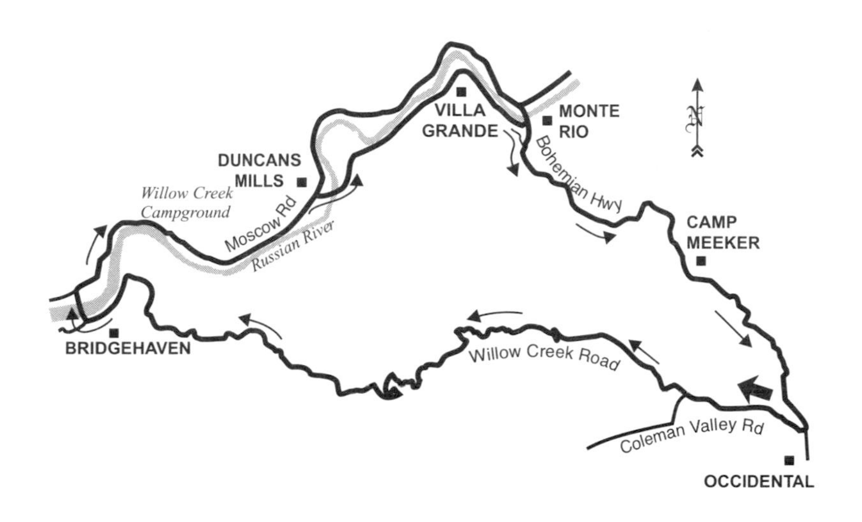
VILLA
GRANDE
MONTE
RIO
N
DUNCANS
MILLS
Willow Creek
Campground
Bohemian Hwy
Moscow Rd
Russian River
CAMP
MEEKER
BRIDGEHAVEN
Willow Creek Road
Coleman Valley Rd
OCCIDENTAL

HIGHWAY 101 ACCESS ROUTE
Cloverdale to Petaluma

REGION: ***NORTHERN SONOMA COUNTY***

MILEAGE: *62 MILES ONE WAY (5-6 Hours Riding Time)*

RATING: *CHALLENGING — This ride is included in the book as an access route for those needing to travel through Sonoma County as part of a tour or as a way of going from one town to another. It is not intended so much as a pleasure ride, but rather as a means to an end.*

ROUTE: *The route described is from north to south, roughly paralleling Highway 101. It begins in the town of Cloverdale and ends at Walnut Park in downtown Petaluma. (Note: If you are planning to travel further south please consult Marin County Bike Trails for a route from Petaluma to the Golden Gate Bridge.)*

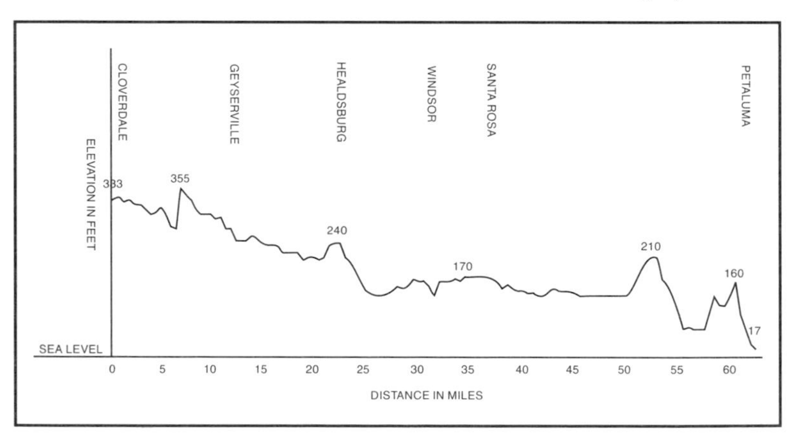

Cloverdale to Geyserville

Begin your trip in downtown Cloverdale, Sonoma County's northernmost town. Take First Street east, which becomes Crocker Road. Cross the bridge over the Russian River and make a sharp right onto River Road for about 5 miles. You will cross a second bridge over the Russian River. This bridge, however, may be closed during winter months due to heavy rain. This road becomes Washington School Road (no signs to indicate this). As an alternate route in the winter months take Asti Road south, which turns into Geyserville Road. Continue on this road to Geyserville.

Geyserville to Healdsburg

In the center of town turn left onto State Highway 128. This is a two-lane country road. You will once again cross the Russian River. Follow it as it winds through lush vineyards. Turn right on River Road (which is still Highway 128) and continue to Alexander Valley (Jimtown). This road also travels smoothly through vineyards on your right and Sulphur Peak on your left.

At the intersection turn right onto Alexander Valley Road where you will again cross the Russian River. At the next intersection continue right to stay on Alexander Valley Road. This road runs into Healdsburg Avenue. At the stop sign bear left and continue south on Healdsburg Avenue to the town of Healdsburg.

Alternate route: This route out of Cloverdale is less desirable because of increasingly heavy traffic, which only lasts for a mile or two. Take South Cloverdale Blvd. and head south. This becomes Dutcher Creek Road and heads west into the rural countryside. Turn left onto Dry Creek Road, which is in a beautiful valley full of lush vineyards. Follow Dry Creek Road to Healdsburg Avenue. Turn right onto Healdsburg Avenue and continue south to the town of Healdsburg.

Healdsburg to Santa Rosa

From Healdsburg you can make several decisions on which route is best for you. This route is more direct and parallels closer to Highway 101. Continue on Healdsburg Avenue, which will turn left near Highway 101. Cross the bridge over the Russian River and ride past Memorial Beach. Turn right and go under the freeway on Old Redwood Highway.

Alternate Route. Westside Road is a longer, but more scenic route, and will take you through some beautiful forested roads. Make a right turn from Healdsburg Avenue onto Westside Road. Follow Westside Road and then take a left onto Wohler Road and cross the Russian River. Take a left again onto River Road and head back toward Old Redwood Highway.

From this point you can choose whether to ride through the downtown section of Santa Rosa or to avoid it and take the back roads on the east side of the freeway.

Santa Rosa to Petaluma

West Side Route. This route parallels the west side of the freeway and avoids downtown Santa Rosa by using the back roads. Old Redwood Highway junctions with Mark West Springs Road (River Road). Turn right and follow River Road for about a mile to the first stoplight after Hwy 101. Turn left onto Fulton Road (heading south). Fulton Road will become South Wright Road. Turn left onto Ludwig Avenue and go to

Stony Point Road. Turn right and follow Stony Point to Gravenstein Highway (116), which is a very busy road. Turn right and follow Stony Point Road to Petaluma Blvd. North. Turn right and continue on to Skillman Lane. Turn right on Skillman Lane.

East Side Route. This route parallels the east side of the freeway and takes you into the heart of downtown Santa Rosa, which may be a preferred route for some. From Old Redwood Highway continue to Santa Rosa and bear left at Mendocino Avenue. Continue along Mendocino Avenue to Santa Rosa Junior College. Turn left onto Pacific Avenue, and then right onto Humboldt. Cross College Avenue. At Fifth Street make a slight jog to the left, then right again onto D Street. Continue to Sonoma Avenue and make a left turn. At Brookwood Avenue turn right. Cross Highway 12 and go past the Sonoma County Fairgrounds. Follow Brookwood as it turns right onto Allan Way. Bear right onto Aston Avenue, and continue past the rows of horse stables. At the stop sign on Petaluma Hill Road turn left.

Continue on Petaluma Hill Road for about 11 miles until you reach the small town of Penngrove. Go through the town to the stop sign at Old Redwood Highway. Turn left onto Old Redwood Highway and follow it for a mile or so. At Ely Road make a left (Caution! This can be a busy intersection). Turn right onto Corona Road and continue over Highway 101 to Petaluma Blvd. North. Cross the boulevard onto Skillman Lane.

At the flashing red light turn left onto Marshall Avenue. Turn right onto Magnolia Avenue and left onto Lohrman Lane. (Caution! There is a blind hill at the intersection.) Turn left onto Bodega Avenue (another busy road). Turn right onto Cleveland Lane, left onto Western Avenue and right at Howard Street (Five Corners), which becomes Sixth Street. Turn left at D Street to get to Walnut Park. From here you can link up with the "Petaluma to the Golden Gate Bridge" ride, described in *Marin County Bike Trails*.

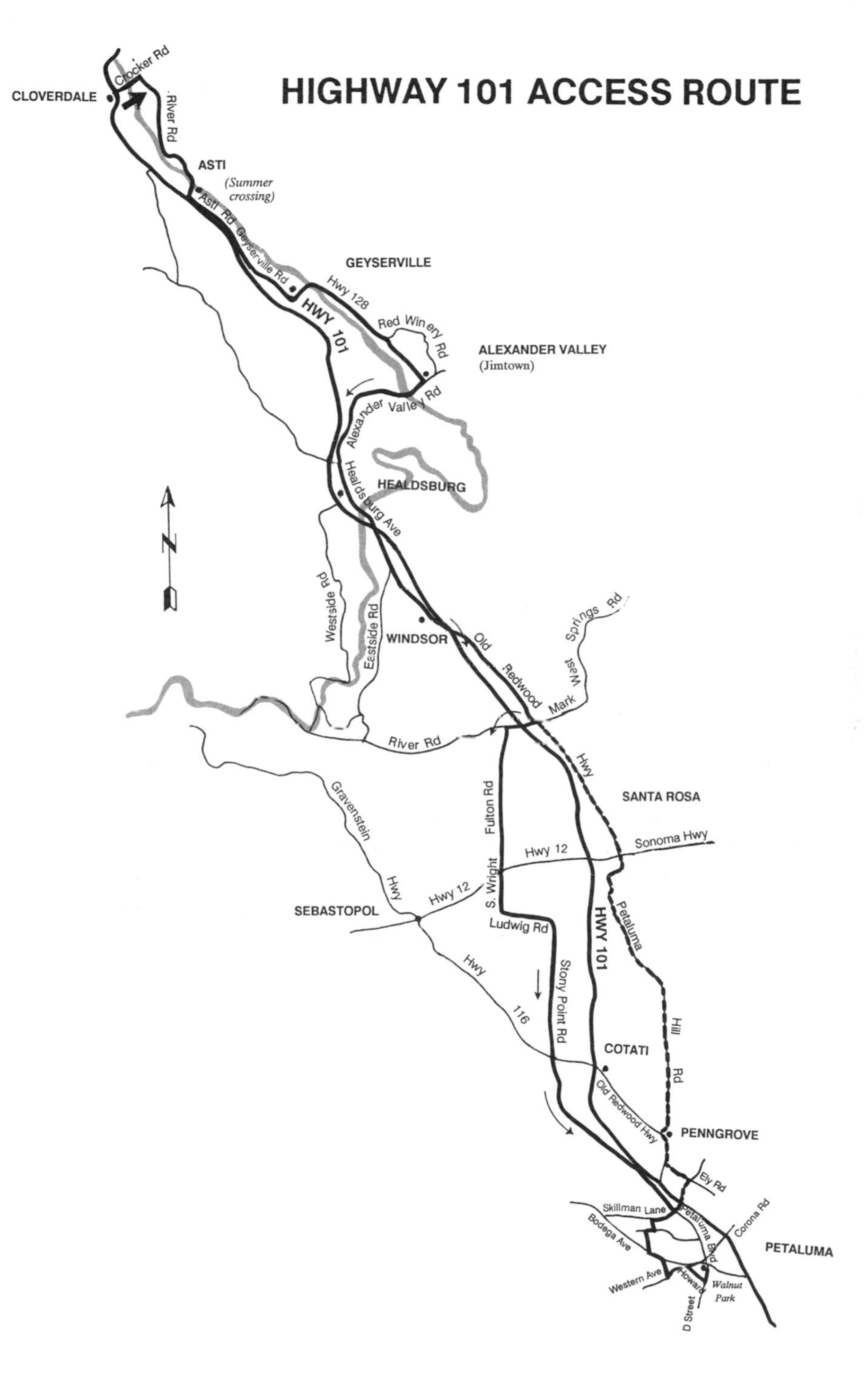
HIGHWAY 101 ACCESS ROUTE
CLOVERDALE
Crocker Rd
River Rd
ASTI
(Summer crossing)
Asti Rd
Geyserville Rd
GEYSERVILLE
Hwy 128
HWY 101
Red Winery Rd
ALEXANDER VALLEY
(Jimtown)
Alexander Valley Rd
HEALDSBURG
Healdsburg Ave
N
Westside Rd
Eastside Rd
WINDSOR
Old Redwood Hwy
Mark West Springs Rd
River Rd
SANTA ROSA
Fulton Rd
Gravenstein Hwy
Hwy 12
Sonoma Hwy
S. Wright
SEBASTOPOL
Ludwig Rd
Hwy 116
Stony Point Rd
Petaluma Hill Rd
COTATI
Old Redwood Hwy
PENNGROVE
Ely Rd
Skillman Lane
Petaluma Blvd
Corona Rd
Bodega Ave
PETALUMA
Western Ave
Howard
Walnut Park
D Street

APPENDIX

RIDES BY RATINGS

EASY RIDES

(short rides, easy grades, good for beginners and children)

3. Penngrove Area Loop Trip (10½ miles) 16
4. City of Sonoma Historic Ramble (11 miles) 20
6. Glen Ellen to Kenwood (10½ miles) 27
9. Cloverdale to Asti (11½ miles) 36
10. Guerneville to Armstrong Woods (6½ miles) 40
17. Santa Rosa — Howarth Park to Spring Lake (5 miles) 66
24. Rohnert Park — Crane Creek Regional Park (7 miles) 91
27. Sebastopol — West County and Joe Rodota Trails (11½ miles) . . 101

MEDIUM RIDES

(longer rides, some hills, not too strenuous)

2. Cotati to Bloomfield (24 miles) 13
5. Sonoma to Glen Ellen (16 miles) 24
7. Healdsburg — Dry Creek Valley (12 miles) 31
8. Geyserville — Alexander Valley Wine Tour (21½ miles) 33
11. Guerneville — River Road Ride (19½ miles) 43
12. Healdsburg — Eastside, Westside Loop (21 miles) 46
13. Monte Rio to Cazadero (20½ miles) 49
18. Santa Rosa — Bennett Valley Loop Trip (15 miles) 69
19. Santa Rosa — Mark West Springs Loop Trip (15 miles) 72
20. Sebastopol — Lone Pine Road Loop Trip (10 miles) 77
22. Occidental to Freestone (9 miles) 83
23. Santa Rosa — Annadel State Park (6½ miles) 88
25. Windsor — Foothill/Shiloh Regional Parks (12 miles) 94
26. Petaluma — Helen Putnam Regional Park (9 miles) 98

CHALLENGING RIDES

(extensive rides with strenuous grades, for more experienced cyclists)

1. Petaluma to the Cheese Factory (21½ miles) 10
14. Bodega to Bodega Head (20 miles) 54
15. Tomales to Valley Ford (17 miles) 58
16. Occidental to the Coast
"The Coleman Valley Experience" (26 miles) 61
21. Freestone–Valley Ford–Bloomfield Triangle (21½ miles) 80
23. Santa Rosa — Annadel State Park (14 miles) 88
28. Occidental — Willow Creek Ride (27 miles) 103

HIGHWAY 101 ACCESS ROUTE 106

BICYCLE SHOPS IN SONOMA COUNTY (1999)

Analy Bike Shop
961 Gravenstein Hwy South
Sebastopol, CA 95472
(707) 823-0425

*Bicycle Factory, The**
110 Kentucky Street
Petaluma, CA 94952
(707) 763-7515

*Bicycle Factory, The**
195 North Main Street
Sebastopol, CA 95444
(707) 829-1880

Bike Hut
917 Golf Course Drive
Rohnert Park, CA 94928
(707) 585-8594

*Bike Peddler, The**
605 College Avenue
Santa Rosa, CA 95404
(707) 571-2428

Cloverdale Cyclery
125 No. Cloverdale Blvd.
Cloverdale, CA 95425
(707) 894-2841

Dave's Bike-Sport
353 College Avenue
Santa Rosa, CA 95401
(707) 528-3283

Gianni Cyclery
3798 Bohemian Hwy
Occidental, CA 95465
(707) 874-2833

*Goodtime Bicycle Company**
18503 Sonoma Hwy
Sonoma, CA 95476
(707) 938-0453

*Healdsburg Spoke Folk Cyclery**
249 Center Street
Healdsburg, CA 95448
(707) 433-7171

*Bicycle Rentals Available

Hub Cyclery, The
7981 Old Redwood Hwy
Cotati, CA 94928
(707) 795-6670

Love Bike, The
234 West Napa Street
Sonoma, CA 95476
(707) 938-2429

Marin Outdoors
2770 Santa Rosa Avenue
Santa Rosa, CA 95401
(707) 544-4400

Mike's Bikes
16442 Main Street
Guerneville, CA 95446
(707) 869-1106

Petaluma Schwinn Cyclery
1080 Petaluma Blvd. No.
Petaluma, CA 94952
(707) 762-1990

Rincon Cyclery
4927 Sonoma Hwy
Santa Rosa, CA 95405
(707) 538-0868

Rohnert Park Cyclery
117 Southwest Blvd.
Rohnert Park, CA 94928
(707) 664-8706

Santa Rosa Cyclery
2300 Midway Drive
Santa Rosa, CA 95404
(707) 522-6232

Sonoma Mountain Cyclery
937 Lakeville Street
Petaluma, CA 94952
(707) 773-3164

Sonoma Valley Cyclery
20093 Broadway
Sonoma, CA 95476
(707) 935-3377

*Sports LTD**
6358 Commerce Blvd.
Rohnert Park, CA 94928
(707) 585-0505

POINTS OF INTEREST (1999)

Bodega Bay

Bodega Marine Laboratory
2099 Westside Road *(707) 875-2211*
Marine life research laboratories run by the University of California. Open all year. One-hour tours on Fridays, 2-4 p.m.

Sonoma Coast State Beaches
Bodega Head to the Russian River
Activities at this 5,000-acre park include picnicking at Wright's Beach and Rock Point, fishing, camping, hiking, horseback riding and surfing.

Cazadero

Berry's Saw Mill
Cazadero Highway and Highway 116 *(707) 865-2365*
Watch trees being processed into lumber. Visitors are free to explore the mill informally. Phone ahead to make sure the mill is operating.

Cloverdale

Bandiera Winery
155 Cherry Creek Road *(707) 894-4295*
Wine-tasting and sales. Open daily 10-5 p.m.

Pastori Winery
23189 Geyserville Avenue *(707) 857-3418*
Pastori Winery has long been a small family winery run by Frank Pastori and his wife, Edith. Open daily 9-5 p.m.; closed major holidays.

Geyserville

Alexander Valley Fruit & Trading Co.
5110 Highway 128 *(707) 433-1944*
A country winery with picnic grounds. Tours available. Open daily 10-5 p.m.

Chateau Souverain
400 Souverain Road *(707) 433-3141*
The Tasting Room and Gift Shop open daily 10-5 p.m. Café At The Winery open daily for lunch, 11:30-2:30 p.m.; dinner Friday-Sunday, 5:30-8:30.

Clos Du Bois Wines
19410 Geyserville Avenue *(707) 857-3100*

Named "Winery of the Year" for the 8th year in a row by Wine & Spirits Magazine. Wine-tasting and sales. Open daily 10-4:30 p.m. Restaurant requires reservations.

Geyser Peak Winery
22281 Chianti Road
(Canyon Road exit off Highway 101) *(707) 897-9463*

Geyserville's first winery. Wines served in tasting room constructed of old redwood tanks and stained glass windows. Picnic areas and hiking trails. Tours by appointment only. Open daily 9-5 p.m.

J. Pedroncelli Winery
1220 Canyon Road *(707) 857-3531*

Bonded in 1904, the original winery and buildings were purchased in 1927 by Giovanni Pedroncelli. Wine-tasting and sales. Tours by appointment only. Open daily 10-5 p.m.

Trentadue Winery
19170 Old Redwood Highway *(707) 433-3104*

A small family winery. Large gift shop and attractive picnic area available. No tours. Open daily 10-5 p.m.

Glen Ellen

Glen Ellen Winery
14301 Arnold Drive *(707) 939-6277*

Established in 1868. Wine-tasting and sales. Tours on weekends. Open daily 9-4:30 p.m.

Jack London State Historic Park
2400 Jack London Ranch Road (near Highway 12) *(707) 938-5216*

Former home of writer, Jack London, this beautiful 800-acre park has miles of rolling hills. "The House of Happy Walls" was built by Mrs. London in 1919 shortly after her husband's death. It stores the collection of South Pacific artifacts, part of London's 18,000-volume library and many of the original furnishing and memorabilia of his life and travels. "The Wolf House" was destroyed by fire in 1913 before the Londons could move in. Only the walls and chimney made of volcanic stone remain. London's grave is nearby, marked by a large boulder.

Valley of the Moon Winery
777 Madrone Road *(707) 996-6941*

Family-owned and operated since 1941. Wine-tasting and sales. Picnic area. Tours by appointment only. Open daily 10-5 p.m.

The World of Jack London
14300 Arnold Drive (near Hill Road) *(707) 996-2888*

This museum, located in the Jack London Book Store, features rare and unusual memorabilia of the California author. Russ Kingman, author of A Pictorial Life of Jack London, offers a slide show and filmstrips.

Guerneville

Armstrong Redwood State Reserve
Armstrong Woods Road (off Highway 116) *(707) 869-2015*

This 752-acre park is home to Sonoma County's oldest and loveliest redwoods. There are picnic areas and walking and hiking trails.

Austin Creek State Recreation Area
17000 Armstrong Woods Road *(707) 869-2015*

Fish, camp, ride horseback or hike at this expansive 4,236-acre park. The Redwood Lake Campground, a rustic area with primitive campsites, is 4 -5-miles from the main road.

Korbel Champagne Cellars
13250 River Road *(707) 887-2294*

World-famous champagne. Elegant tasting room and picnic area. Tours every 45 minutes, 9:30-4 p.m. Open daily 9-5 p.m.

Healdsburg

Alexander Valley Vineyards
8644 Highway 128 *(707) 433-7209*

The vineyard and winery are located on the original homestead of Cyrus Alexander, dating from the 1840's. Open daily 10-5 p.m.

Belvedere Wine Company
4035 Westside Road *(707) 433-8236*

Wine-tasting and sales. Picnic area. Tours by appointment only. Open Monday through Saturday, 10-4:30 p.m.

Congressman Don Clausen Fish Hatchery
3246 Skaggs Springs Road *(707) 433-6325*

Built to protect the migrating silver salmon and steelhead trout because of the construction of the Dry Creek Dam. It also raises king salmon. The hatchery is operated by the California Department of Fish and Game.

Davis Bynum Winery
8075 Westside Road *(707) 433-5852*

Set in a country atmosphere of lush vineyards and hills along Westside Road. Wine-tasting and sales. Picnic grounds. Open daily 10-5 p.m.

Dry Creek Vineyard
3770 Lambert Bridge Road *(707) 433-1000*

Built in the 1840's, the winery was the original home of Cyrus Alexander. Friendly, informal atmosphere and pleasant picnic grounds. Tours by appointment only. Open daily 10:30-4:30 p.m.

Field Stone Winery & Vineyard
10075 Highway 128 *(707) 433-7266*

Beautiful picnic area. Summer evening concerts. Wine-tasting and sales. Open daily 10-5 p.m.

Foppiano Vineyards
12707 Old Redwood Highway *(707) 433-7272*

Founded in 1896, this winery has the longest history of family ownership and operation in Sonoma County. Wine-tasting and sales. Tours by appointment only. Open daily 10-4:30 p.m.

Healdsburg Memorial Beach Park
Healdsburg Avenue (near Front Street) *(707) 433-1625*

This popular park features a beach with lifeguards two diving boards and a boat launching pad, snack bars and a picnic area. Restrooms are available.

Hop Kiln Winery
6050 Westside Road *(707) 433-6491*

Restored in 1905, this winery is set on 240 acres, and is a state historic landmark and the site of several movies. Historic tasting room in landmark hops barn and picnic area. Open daily 10-5 p.m.

Johnson's Alexander Valley Wines
8333 Highway 128 *(707) 433-2319*

Built in the 1930's. Open house and concerts once a month. Occasional theater pipe organ concerts. Picnic tables. Wine-tasting and sales. Open daily 10-5 p.m.

Lake Sonoma and Warm Springs Dam
Dry Creek Road (at Rockpile Road)

The 319-foot-high Warm Springs Dam, designed to control Russian River flooding, is the largest structure ever built in Sonoma County. The Visitors' Center has exhibits about the dam and the history of the region.

Lambert Bridge Winery
4085 West Dry Creek Road *(707) 431-9600*

Wine-tasting and sales. Open daily 10-4:30 p.m.

Mill Creek Vineyards & Winery
1401 Westside Road *(707) 433-5098*

Wine-tasting and sales. Picnic area. Open daily 10-4:30 p.m.

Preston Vineyards & Winery
9206 West Dry Creek Road *(707) 433-3372*

Retail sales Monday through , 11-3 p.m.

Ridge/Lytton Springs Winery
640 Lytton Springs Road *(707) 433-7721*

Wine-tasting and sales. Tours by appointment only. Open daily 10-4 p.m.

Rodney Strong Vineyards
11455 Old Redwood Highway *(707) 431-1533*

Founded in 1959, the winery features concerts and cultural events throughout the summer. Picnic in Greek theater. Depending on the time of the year, you can get hands-on experience pruning vines, sugar-testing grapes, or even a crash course on evaluating wines right out of the barrel. Tours 11 a.m. and 3 p.m. during summer. Open daily 10-5 p.m.

Sausal Winery
7370 Highway 128 *(707) 433-2285*

Alexander Valley's oldest winemaking family. Tasting room. Tours by appointment only. Open daily 10-4 p.m.

Simi Winery
16275 Healdsburg Avenue *(707) 433-6981*

Founded over a century ago. Wine-tasting and sales. Picnic area. Tours at 11 a.m., 1 and 3 p.m. Open daily 10-4:30 p.m.

Kenwood

Chateau St. Jean Vineyards
8555 Sonoma Highway *(707) 833-4134*

Wine-tasting and sales. Self-guided tour of the fermentation cellar and crush area. Picnic grounds. Open daily 10:30-4 p.m.

Kenwood Vineyard & Winery
9592 Sonoma Highway *(707) 833-5891*

Rustic tasting room. Tours by appointment only. Open daily 10-4:30 p.m.

Morton's Warm Spring Recreation Park
1651 Warm Springs Road *(707) 833-5511*

The park has two swimming pools, a wading pool, a softball field, horseshoe pits, a volleyball court, snack bar and picnic area with barbecue pits. Open daily May through September, 9-6 p.m. Closed winter.

Smothers Brothers/Remick Ridge Vineyards
9575 Sonoma Highway *(707) 833-1010*

Owned and operated by the famous Smothers Brothers comedy team. Tasting room housed in rustic cabin. Open daily 10-4:30 p.m.

Sugarloaf Ridge State Park
2605 Adobe Canyon Road (near Highway 12) *(707) 833-5712*

Popular activities at this 2,373-acre park include camping, picnicking, hiking and horse-back riding. A lodge provides food and drinks and a place to relax.

Petaluma

The Creamery Store
711 Western Avenue (at Baker) *(707) 778-1234*

Petaluma cheeses, gifts, picnic area. Tour of cheese plant, slide show from 10:30 a.m. Open Monday-Friday 10-6 p.m; Saturday 10-5 p.m.

Marin French Cheese Company
7500 Red Hill Road *(707) 762-6001*

Manufacturer of French cheeses: Camembert, Brie, Breakfast and Schloss. Picnic area, lagoon with piped-in background classical music and picnic supplies. 15-minute tours of the cheese plant from 10-4 p.m. Open daily 9-5 p.m.

Petaluma Adobe Historic State Park
3325 Adobe Road (at Casa Grande Road) *(707) 762-4871*

General Mariano Vallejo's Petaluma Rancho, built in 1840, is now open as a museum. Outdoor displays include cowhide racks, the old forge, and large ovens where bread was baked for the Rancho inhabitants.

Petaluma Historic Museum and Library
20 Fourth Street (at B Street) *(707) 778-4398*

Open Thursday through Monday 1-4 p.m.

Santa Rosa

Annadel State Park
6201 Channel Drive (off Montgomery Drive) *(707) 539-3911*

This 4,913-acre park features hiking, biking and horseback riding trails, nature walks and exhibits. Visitors can fish at Lake Ilsanjo, and Ledson Marsh offers wildlife viewing.

Crane & Sons Melons
4947 Petaluma Hill Road *(707) 584-5141*

Home of the original Crane melons, which are in season September 1st. The store sells melons, tomatoes, corn and squash in season. Open daily August 15 through November 15, 10-6 p.m.

Hood Mountain Regional Park
3000 Los Alamos Drive (east from Highway 12) *(707) 527-2041*

This 1,450-acre park has lovely vistas from the top of the steep trail, as well as on the way up. Closed during fire season (mainly summer).

Howarth Memorial Park
Summerfield Road (near Montgomery Drive)

This 152-acre park offers boat rentals, six tennis courts, a softball field, picnic and barbecue areas, a large playground as well as bicycle, horse and jogging trails. There is a petting zoo, and visitors can feed the ducks at Lake Ralphine.

Luther Burbank Memorial Gardens
204 Santa Rosa Avenue (and Sonoma Avenue)

In his 53-years residence in Santa Rosa Luther Burbank developed over 300 plant varieties, including more than 25 marketable vegetables and over 250 varieties of fruits. This national Historical Landmark features experimental gardens once used by the "Plant Wizard," as well as his home with its reflecting pool and greenhouse.

Pacific Coast Air Museum
2330 Airport Blvd. *(707) 575-7900*

Antique World War II airplanes. Open Tuesday-Thursday 10-2 p.m.; weekends 10-4 p.m.

Petrified Forest
4100 Petrified Forest Road, Calistoga *(707) 942-6667*

Open since 1870. Several ancient petrified trees, many over 100 feet tall, have been unearthed here for display. Covered by volcanic ash when Mt. St. Helena erupted 6 million years ago, the trees are now in unusual formations and colors. Petrified sea shells, clams and marine life can be seen here as well. Museum, picnic grounds and gift shop.

Ripley's Memorial Museum ("Church of One Tree")
492 Sonoma Avenue and Santa Rosa Avenue *(707) 524-5233*

Dedicated to the unusual and incredible, the museum is housed in a strange and beautiful church built from the planks and boards of a single giant redwood tree. Closed from December to February.

Sonoma County Museum
425 Seventh Street (at B Street) *(707) 579-1500*

Artifacts and displays documenting the cultural history of Sonoma county and Northern California are exhibited here.

Sonoma County Parks Department
2300 County Center Drive *(707) 539-2865*

Spring Lake County Park
Newanga Avenue and Summerfield Road *(707) 539-8082*

Popular activities at this 320-acre park include non-motorized boating, swimming, fishing, camping, and picnicking.

Sebastopol

Ragle Ranch Park
Ragle Road (off Bodega Highway) *(707) 823-7262*

This 156-acre day-use park, once the Ragle family ranch and still family-owned, offers hiking, biking and equestrian trails.

Sonoma

Bartholomew Park Winery
1000 Vineyard Lane *(707) 935-9511*

Wine-tasting and sales. Wine garden for picnics overlooking vineyard and pond. Tours by appointment only. Open daily 10-5 p.m.

Buena Vista Winery
18000 Old Winery Road *(707) 938-1266*

Oldest premium winery in California, built in 1857. State Historic Landmark. Art gallery. Large picnic area. Wine-tasting and sales in historic Press House. Self-guided tours of wine caves. Open daily 10-4:30 p.m.

Depot Park Historical Museum
210 First Street West *(707) 938-1762*

Open Wednesdays through Sundays, 1-4 p.m.

Gundlach-Bundschu Winery
2000 Denmark Street *(707) 938-5277*

Award-winning picturesque winery. Only U.S. producer of Kleinberger. Picnic hill with great views. Nature hike. Wine-tasting and sales. Self-guided tour. Open daily 11-4:30 p.m.

Ravenswood Winery
18701 Gehricke Road *(707) 938-1960*

Wine-tasting and sales. Tours by appointment only. Open daily 10-4:30 p.m.

Sebastiani Vineyards
389 Fourth Street East *(707) 938-5532*

Extensive Indian artifact collection and largest collection of hand-carved casks in California. Guided tours 10-4:20 p.m. Wine-tasting and sales. Open daily 10-4:30 p.m.

Sonoma Cheese Factory
2 Spain Street (on the Plaza) *(707) 996-1000*

Home of Sonoma Jack Cheese. Large deli, wines, picnic items, outdoor eating, factory viewing, slide presentation on cheese-making, samples. Open daily 9-6 p.m.

Sonoma State Historic Park Mission
and Vallejo Home and Barracks
Third Street West at Spain Street (on the Plaza) *(707) 938-1519*

Once the northernmost town of the Mexican empire, Sonoma has a number of historically significant structures: the sites of General Vallejo's two Sonoma homes and Mission San Francisco Solano de Sonoma. Open daily 9-5 p.m.

Train Town
20264 Broadway Avenue *(707) 938-3912*

Ten acre railroad park. Steam trains travel through 10 acres of landscaped park filled with trees, lakes, bridges, tunnels and reconstructed historic structures. 15-minute train trip; refreshments. Open daily weekends and holidays June through Labor Day, 10:30-5:30 p.m.

Vella Cheese Company
315 Second Street East *(707) 938-3232*

Observe the cheese-making process on days of production. Open Monday through Saturday 9-6 p.m; Sunday 10-5 p.m.

Windsor

Windsor Waterworks and Slides
8225 Conde Lane (near Old Redwood Highway) *(707) 838-7760*

Slide and splash at this water park which features "The Doom Flume" and other water slides. There are also a swimming pool, wading pool, game room, snack bar and picnic area.

THE BAY AREA BIKE TRAILS SERIES

The Bay Area Bike Trails Series offers over 175 self-guided road and mountain bicycle tours. Each ride contains clear, detailed maps, easily followed directions with mile markers, elevation profiles of the terrain, beautiful photographs, historical background and points of interest.

Bay Area Mountain Bike Trails by Conrad J. Boisvert, 1993 (latest revision 1995). $13.95. The Bay Area offers some of the most exciting and scenic off-road trails and a wealth of hidden trails, all within easy access of major cities. From Santa Rosa south to Gilroy, you can ride along the spectacular ridges of Mt. Tamalpais, view the Golden Gate Bridge from the Marin Headlands, or challenge yourself on the hills of Mt. Diablo.

East Bay Bike Trails by Conrad J. Boisvert, 1992 (latest revision 1993). $12.95. Somewhat sheltered from coastal fog and ocean winds, the East Bay extends from the Carquinez Strait south to Fremont. Interesting bike routes take you through heavily wooded hills above Oakland and Berkeley, orchards and farms around Brentwood, eerie windmills in Livermore, the wetlands around Newark, and dramatic Mount Diablo in Danville.

Marin County Bike Trails by Phyllis L. Neumann, 1989 (latest revision 1996). $12.95. Just across the Golden Gate Bridge, Marin County combines exquisite natural beauty with sophisticated elegance to give you spectacular views, rugged cliffs, natural beaches, well-developed parks, rural farmlands, tiny hidden towns and Mt. Tamalpais. A specially designed bike route from Petaluma to the Golden Gate Bridge is also included.

San Francisco Peninsula Bike Trails by Conrad J. Boisvert, 1991 (latest revision 1993). $11.95. Few areas can compare with the spectacular San Francisco Peninsula, which encompasses the wooded foothills around Woodside, dense redwood forests in the Santa Cruz mountains and remote country roads along the rugged Pacific coastline.

Sonoma County Bike Trails by Phyllis L. Neumann, 1978 (3rd Edition 1999). $13.95. Less than an hour's drive north from San Francisco brings you to tranquil country roads, gently rolling farmlands, towering redwoods, lush vineyards, local wineries, the Russian River and the Pacific coastline. A specially designed bike route from Cloverdale to Petaluma is also included.

South Bay Bike Trails by Conrad J. Boisvert, 1990 (2nd Edition 1999). $13.95. Better known for its high-tech image, once you head out into the surrounding countryside, the South Bay is a cyclist's paradise. From San Jose south to Gilroy, picturesque rides take you through ranchlands around Morgan Hill, dense redwood forests in the Santa Cruz mountains, and the coastal wetlands of the Elkhorn Slough. Heading south along the Pacific coast brings you to the famous seaside resorts and beaches of Santa Cruz and Capitola.